# CONTENTS P9-DHL-321

PREFACE TO THE ENGLISH EDITION

VII


PROLOGUE

IX

CHAPTER ONE

A LETTER OF OFFERING TO TRUE PARENTS

1


CHAPTER TWO

EARTHLY LIFE
AND LIFE IN THE SPIRIT WORLD

7


CHAPTER THREE

LIFE IN THE SPIRIT WORLD
VIEWED FROM THE PRINCIPLE

47


CHAPTER FOUR

MEETINGS IN THE SPIRIT WORLD I

77


CHAPTER FIVE

MEETINGS IN THE SPIRIT WORLD II

107

# LIFE IN THE SPIRIT WORLD AND ON EARTH

# LIFE IN THE SPIRIT WORLD AND ON EARTH

## MESSAGES FROM THE SPIRIT WORLD

## DR. SANG HUN LEE

FAMILY FEDERATION
. FOR WORLD PEACE
AND UNIFICATION

FAMILY FEDERATION FOR WORLD PEACE AND UNIFICATION

4 West 43rd Street
New York, NY 10036

© 1998 by Family Federation for World Peace and Unification

ISBN 0-910621-90-X

# PREFACE TO THE ENGLISH EDITION

Dr. Sang Hun Lee, who passed into spirit world at age 84 on 22 March, 1997, is known for his work in philosophy, economics and social theory. A rigorous intellectual, throughout his life he also was acutely interested in the nature of the spirit world. He felt it most important that clear knowledge of spirit world be available in the physical world. This interest remained with him through his time of transition and resulted in this book.

Sang Hun Lee was born in 1914 in Korea. He gained his license as a physician from Severance Medical School (now Yonsei University Medical School), Seoul, Korea. In the mid-1950s, he and his wife joined the Unification Church. Dr. Lee set aside his medical practice and devoted himself to scholarly expression of Reverend Moon's thought. He in fact did not want his own viewpoint to distort the clear teachings of his spiritual leader. In 1992, he wrote, "Quite a few scholars began to think that the content of those books was the author's own thought, even though the author had clearly introduced them as Rev. Moon's thought. That misunderstanding deeply grieved the author's heart."

Dr. Lee's first works dealt with Marxism-Leninism. South Korea, faced with the threat of invasion from the North, had banned discussion of communist theory. In a state of ignorance, the people had no real defense against Marxist ideas. Reverend Moon recognized the necessity of an critical response to Marxism, and guided Dr. Lee's work to this end. It was difficult for Dr. Lee to obtain texts on Marxism in that era. Nonetheless, at some personal risk, he obtained books and wrote *Communism: A Critique and Counterproposal*. To the satisfaction of all, the South Korean government approved the text for the education of its citizenry. The work formed the core of ideas developed later in the CAUSA worldview, which had worldwide impact in the struggle for freedom in the 1980s.

Dr. Lee moved on to the philosophical implications of Reverend Moon's teachings. His careful inheritance of his teacher's thought resulted in a series of books on "Unification Thought." Here, Dr. Lee applied Rev. Moon's teachings to the questions asked by philosophers: what is the purpose of life? What is a good life? What constitutes the good society? How do we ascertain truth? How do we measure value? He assessed the contributions of the major philosophers from the Greeks to the present-day, and offered the Unificationist solution to their knotty problems.

Dr. Lee always had a practical goal: the alleviation of human suffering, and attainment of human happiness. His recent books and seminars on "Headwing Thought" and "Godism" provided a foundation for development of Unification education in true family values. His work thus serves as a foundation for the expansion of God's blessing upon marriages of all faiths and societies around the world.

With a number of his students, Dr. Lee established the Unification Thought Institute in Seoul, with branch offices in Tokyo and New York City.

By way of explanation, Mrs. Young Soon Kim is the medium, or "reporter," of Dr. Lee's messages from spirit world. She is a Unificationist elder and church leader. Her prologue is to this book's first four chapters, which she received in 1997 and which were published in Korean and Japanese editions. She received the fifth chapter in May of 1998, and it is included in the English edition.

Dr. Tyler Hendricks
Vice-President
Family Federation for World Peace and Unification America

# PROLOGUE

Let me start with a very old story regarding the late Dr. Lee. This is the story when our couple was doing ministerial work. Among our congregation, there were many professors who had grizzled hair. Even though I was not the speaker, when my husband was giving a sermon before such intellectual members, I was so tense that my hands were wet with perspiration. On Sunday, we usually spent time managing various office jobs after Sunday service. As usual, after finishing my office work, when I was leaving the church late one Sunday, Dr. Lee was waiting for me at the entrance of the church. When I asked why he had waited for me, he pulled out something from his pocket and shyly gave it to me. It was a cake of soap which he had bought during his overseas trip.

At this moment as I am going to write the prologue of this book, old memories about the late Dr. Lee come back to my mind. With this remembrance, my mind comes to be filled with yearning and respect for him. Dr. Lee always gave our couple deep love and concern. Moreover, he lived a lonely life for eight years after his wife's death. One day, he called me to his house and gave me a big box, saying, "Because I am healthy, please eat this and work very hard for the sake of God." That gift was what someone had presented to Dr. Lee. When I think about the gift again, my cheeks burn with shame because I received it and ate as though I did not know how to eat and even had not seen it. I still don't know whether having received that gift was good or not. At that time, I could not express my opinion or feeling freely before Dr. Lee because he was a very respectable person to me. He often invited us to his office at the Unification Thought Institute. Whenever I went there, I always felt awkward before him. The reason is that even though Dr. Lee was an elder, he treated us very politely and courteously. When we visited his office, he always gave us a warm welcome.

His wife was also very polite and kind to us. She always bowed very politely and courteously to us who were very young like her children. When she was talking to us, she always used terms of respect. Since she was the same age as my mother, I sincerely asked her to treat me like her daughter. However, she said, "Because this courteous attitude is a habit, I feel more comfortable to do so." They were admirable persons who became habituated to respect others and use terms of respect. I want to keep them in my heart as beautiful and respectable persons eternally.

When Dr. Lee was living in this physical world, he said that with Divine Principle, he could answer every question at an academic seminar, but he could not give a clear answer about questions regarding the spirit world. Therefore, he said that some day, he would necessarily complete the doctrine of the spirit world. He studied the spirit world through every material such as "Great Spirit World," "Hwa Bo" which were testified by spiritual persons. Moreover, because his wife was in the spiritual world, he gave some questions to ask to his wife. He wanted to know what his wife saw in the spiritual world.

Dr. Lee continuously gave me many questions regarding the spirit world. However, it took time until I got an answer through prayer, and a lot of physical energy was required in praying. Questioning and getting answers by prayer were repeated continuously. However, because of my busy life, I could not pray deeply to get answer from the spirit world. So, there was one time that several months passed without receiving an answer. Dr. Lee also did not urge me to get an answer.

About the time when I came to think that he might have forgotten, he sent a message to me that said, "Even though the answer for my question is late in coming, I can understand your situation. If it is possible, you can give me the answer slowly." I would like to express again my deep respect for his benevolence and tenacity. Despite his desperate efforts, he passed from his life without completing the doctrine of the spirit world. When I attended the Seung Hwa ceremony, I felt my heart was broken. However, at that time, the late Dr. Lee appeared to me and said, "Since this is a solemn time, I cannot speak to you. I will go to your house this evening."

When I was wondering if the late Dr. Lee who had died just now could go to my house, God said, "Sang Hun is a man of the Kingdom of Heaven." I was surprised. "A man of the Kingdom of Heaven?" I was hearing that name for the first time. One whom God admits is a man of the Kingdom of Heaven, is the very person whom I thought was also. I was very happy because my feeling for Dr. Lee was right

Since that night, the late Dr. Lee came to our house day and night. No matter what I was doing, he appeared to me and urged me to do his work. I struggled so much over that. Thus, I complained to God saying, "God! It is too much for me. I cannot endure any more. If you say that Sang Hun Lee is a man of the Kingdom of Heaven, then am I a woman of the Hell? How can things be done like this? I can't do any more." God said that "My daughter! Because Sang Hun is my son, I want to let him do as he wants. Now, He is very busy in this spirit world. Because he is looking around the spirit world which he was most anxious to know about during his life time, how busy his mind is! He wants to tell about what he studied and analyzed in the spirit world. He is going to look all around the physical world as well as the spirit world. Therefore, please understand his situation." So, I said to God again, crying "Then, how can my physical body endure this hard work?" The late Dr. Lee said, "My daughter! Let's make a time schedule and let's do according to that." He promised that he would not come except during the appointed time.

The next day, he came and said, "Mrs. Kim! You would suffer in working with me. However, please understand my earnest situation to inform people of the reality of the spirit world." Contrary to his ordinary attitude, he seemed to talk like a mere child. Therefore, I doubted if he was the real Dr. Lee. So Dr. Lee said, "My feelings are hurt." He added that after surveying the spirit world for 40 days, he would tell me all his findings in detail.

At that time, we were very busy preparing to go to Australia. When I told him that we were going there, he said that he would come too. We consequently went there and were working hard to adapt to our new surroundings. We almost forgot Dr. Lee's words. One day, however, Dr. Lee came to us angrily. He complained because even though 40 days had already passed, we did not find him.

He said, "Please forgive and understand me for being so excited. Because this spirit world is a new world to me, I was very busy systematizing what I had to study. I was too excited and moved very much. Moreover, since I wanted to tell these things to the physical world as soon as possible, I forgot my manners. Please forgive and understand me." He came back to his ordinary frame of mind.

Where shall we start? I was wondering how he would work with me. I was also afraid how long he would continue to do this. However, since I was already involved, I began by asking God to give me power and courage. Every word, which he gave to me until now, was very valuable. In this prologue,

I am going to talk about some of the points which greatly affected me.

In the eternal world where our members are staying, if it is not a special case, every member lives close to God with each one's committed sin visible. That seems to be very severe punishment. How can we say that is the kingdom of heaven? That seems to be a more fearful place than Hell.

Next, I am going to talk about couple's love. Since a couple become one through love, the couple's lives themselves are the substantial body of love. Their love is to give joy to God. When they make love in the field of flowers, on waves, on the blue grass, in the mountain where birds are singing, and in the midst of a forest, all surroundings will dance and be harmonized with them. Moreover, God's beautiful and brilliant light twirls around them, which we can never imagine with our practical minds.

However, the couple who did not become one can love only in their bedroom even in the spirit world. If any one side did not become complete or has a defect, the other side has to wait until that side becomes perfect. But that is an endless time, which cannot be guaranteed. That is also the period of fearful punishment and the time of judgment.

What is the motivation of the fall of Lucifer and Eve? We thought that they just fell. Until the time when the crisis of the fall came, Lucifer took the young Eve along with him. The bud of love with Eve grew and finally he fell in love with her. Adam did not recognize what was happening. Since that time, the relationship between Adam and Eve became much more serious than we think. Although Eve did not forget her first love with Lucifer, she could not but rely on Adam because of fear and uneasiness. Therefore, can you imagine how their couple's love was?

Next, I am going to speak about Kim, Il Sung whom he had met in the spirit world. Kim, Il Sung was moved by Dr. Lee's heartistic and tearful lecture and love. Even though when he was living in the physical world he had absolute power and authority, in the spirit world he was expelled even from the bottom of the Hell. He is in the miserable situation of having to wait for salvation at the doorsill. How shall we live our lives during our earthly lives? It is fearful. There are many surprising things.

We drink water after cleansing it through a water purifier. However, even though we cleanse ourselves more than that, it is difficult for us to stand before God in the eternal world. Because there is no law of indemnity in the spirit world, if one committed sin during one's earthly life, one always has to stay at the same position no matter how many thousand years have passed. Moreover, if one committed sin and is staying in hell, the future way of one's descendants comes to be blocked. How painful and sad a fact this is!

Here, I come to think of a question. When True Father goes to the spirit world, if my most beloved son fell into hell and was struggling, shall he save him? Otherwise, because of the law of the spirit world, shall he just wait? Thus, if one commits sin in the physical world, that would be another impiety to True Parents.

Even though every word which Dr. Lee spoke was new and surprised me, I doubted if he was really Dr. Lee many times. The reason is because when he begins to speak, he starts from the same contents of the Divine Principle. Whenever I doubted him, he got very angry. He said "My pride is hurt. I am Sang Hun Lee who systematized Unification Thought. Because there is not enough time to talk and I have many things to speak, I have to be patient. Let's begin quickly." Saying that, he became calm and urged me to begin. So far, while I was reporting, his daughter asked individual questions regarding their family many times, but he did not answer anything about that. If his daughter tried to beg earnestly, he left. During the time of reporting, he appeared only publicly, saying that he had no time to talk about his family.

When I got tired of reporting, he said, "Let's take a break for a minute and drink a cup of coffee." Dr. Lee was very detailed. He was worried about my health, saying, "Please exercise your arm and move it. If you feel it is too hard, let's finish early. Let's call it a day." He consoled me like this. When our work was finished, if I asked what he would speak about the next day, he did not answer and just left. Likewise, his character also had a cool side. Even though I asked many times how many days he is going to continue, he did not answer even once. When it was just two days short of three months since his first report, he only said, "Let's reduce time and do a little bit more." And then, he continued to report without mentioning any thing about the period of report. At 10 o'clock of the final day of the three months, Dr. Lee was crying very much while giving the last letter.

"Mrs. Kim! Thank you for your hard work. I don't know if I can be a help to True Parents. When I came here and saw this world, I found out that this world is very vast. I don't know how I can explain about this world. If I do not report about this world to the physical world, that seems to give more burden to True Parents. So, I tried to do my best. Don't you know how much our members worked hard in this physical world? Despite that, if our members come to this spirit world and have a hard time, that would make God's heart painful and cause anxiety to True Parents. Therefore, I wish you to teach many members to live right lives while on earth. Then they will not go to the middle or dark spirit world, but close to God. I would like to ask you to read this letter in detail. Please tell intellectuals that they should study their major field as well as the lives of the spirit world. This spirit world is not the place where one can come to God by being proud of one's intellect or major." He cried a great deal while saying this. When he finished this report and left us, his appearance from behind looked very sad and heavy. He went walking very slowly.

In reporting his letter, I would like to express my deep appreciation and respect for Dr. Lee's efforts. He spoke systematically and in detail. The content of this book was given by Dr. Lee who died in March, 1997, and was written with the purpose to teach earthly people urgently about the reality of the spirit world and the heavenly value of True Parents. Therefore, this book did not mention about the providence of True Parents on earth or Chung Pyung's providence by Dae Mo Nim and the Holy Spirit. I am expecting more graceful contents.

I finish this report with sincere wishes that this letter can be helpful to you as Dr. Lee loves every member.

Young Soon Kim
*Sydney, Australia*

CHAPTER ONE

# A LETTER OF OFFERING TO TRUE PARENTS

# THE LETTER TO TRUE PARENTS

*(Dr. Lee began with praying "True Parents! I hope you can be consoled by my letter.")*

True Parents! I would like to give my best regards to you. I hope to receive your love and forgiveness because of the impiety of my earthly life. I cannot but feel sad before True Parents because I came here to the spirit world prior to you.

I know very well the continuous, desperate efforts of the True Parents to successfully fulfill the 3.6 million couple international Blessing. In the spirit world, our members are also working very hard to witness to people. However, even though we make strenuous effort to restore the spirit world, many fundamental problems can be resolved only when you come. I am very sorry for that because it will cause you trouble.

Since True Father will conduct the Blessing in spirit world, multitudes are waiting for you. Now, we lecture that the door of hell will be opened and hell will be liberated. However, even though we try to do our best, it cannot be compared with our True Father's efforts. We desire and pray that our small efforts can reduce your burden.

True Parents! When I lived in the physical world, intellectuals often asked me about the spirit world, but I could not knowledgeably answer. Whenever we held academic seminars, people asked about the spirit world. But I could not give a clear answer. The spirit world was like a riddle that I could not solve by myself. Accordingly, without first systematizing the doctrine of the spirit world, I came here. Therefore, for the following reasons I will try to carefully relate details about the spirit world: First, I want to solve many of the questions troubling earthly people. Second, I want to assist our Unification members while on Earth to live properly. Third, even though my efforts are very small, I want to reduce our True Parents' trouble. Fourth, I am bothered by a guilty conscience because I came to the spirit world prior to True Father.

True Father! So far, your humble son, Sang Hun, has explored various areas of the spirit world. As long as it is possible, I want to search all around the spirit world. Now, I am going to relate what I have surveyed in the spirit world. If my message contains error, please blame me and correct it. It is my sincere heart to help members by revealing the secrets of the spirit world. I hope that by knowing the spirit world, people living in the physical world will not commit sin, and will come to the spirit world without sin. By doing so, I pray that our True Father's burden will be reduced when he comes to spirit world. Moreover, God is burdened and poor.

True Father! I would like to deeply express appreciation for sending me to this blessed place, and giving me the title, "Blessed Man." After completing my earthly life with your grace and blessing, I came to the spirit world. So, I will sincerely devote myself to liberate hell in this eternal world.

True Father and True Mother! As a blessed couple we ask for your forgiveness because we live comfortably in the spirit world. We would like to offer a full bow in front of True Parents. May True Parents live long lives!

—August 21, 1997, Sang Hun

## TO BELOVED MEMBERS
## OF THE UNIFICATION CHURCH

"I would like to offer this letter to our beloved members."

Dear members! What shall I write first? No one can avoid physical death nor escape the spirit world. It is the way of Heavenly law through which everyone must pass. I miss our members of Unification Church since I came to the spirit world. I am really concerned about how to educate all members not to violate Heavenly law in the physical world so that you will be able to pass smoothly into the spirit world. If you violate the law of the spirit world, you cannot solve it easily, and you will pay the price of indemnity through suffering in the spirit world. Beloved members of the Unification Church! What a hard time you have had! I desire that when you arrive in this eternal world, you can live happily. I wish that you would not try to escape temporary hard times. If you persevere, you will find eternal life.

If you violate Heavenly law, your descendants will have to pay indemnity instead of you. When True Parents organize the spirit world, your wrong behavior will pain the True Parents' heart. Dear members of the Unification Church! My name is Sang Hun Lee, who wrote Unification Thought. I am going to relate what I surveyed in the spirit world. Please read it carefully, and make your earthly lives successful. By doing so, let's console the painful heart of True Parents, and pray that True Parents may have long lives. Please read my message very carefully. You should measure your lives every day by the standard of True Parents' speech. This is my advice as your elder brother, to help you fulfill your responsibility successfully on earth. May God bless all of you!

—August 21, 1997 From Sang Hun

CHAPTER TWO

# EARTHLY LIFE
# AND
# LIFE IN THE SPIRIT WORLD

# MEETING AT THE SEUNG HWA CEREMONY
# OF SANG HUN LEE                    *MARCH 24, 1997*

## *My Name Is Sang Hun Lee*

Please don't try to test who I am. It creates a bad feeling in me. I had wanted to meet you more often during my earthly life. However, it was not easy to meet each other. Dear Mrs. Kim! Through you, I am going to complete what I did not complete during my earthly life. Please don't say that you have no any qualifications to do that.

## *Unification Thought Is*
## *the Fundamental Thought*

Unification Thought is the fundamental thought that True Father gave us, but many people try to understand it just intellectually. Therefore, throughout my whole lifetime in the physical world, I was trying to write many books to help people more easily understand Unification Thought. However, I could not completely fulfill that. Therefore, from the spirit world, I am going to send you what I did not complete in the physical world, so that you can share it with all people.

Mrs. Kim! From my earthly life, I know that you worked very hard. Therefore, from now on, I am going to help you centering on Rev. Ho Woong Chung's family in the spirit world. Please, wait for this. Even though God said that I don't need to stay on earth for 40 days, I will go around the earth as well as the spirit world as far as I can, so that I can systematize my thought and relate that to you. My wife also has many things to share with you. Mrs. Kim! Even though for a while you may feel troubled because of me, please forgive me. After putting my thoughts in order for 40 days, I will return. Although you may go to Australia, I can go there. Then, I will visit you again. Thank you.

Also, I would like to express my appreciation because everyone beautifully eulogized me in the Seung Hwa ceremony.

## MEMORIAL SERVICE AT HIS HOME
## WITH HIS FAMILY MEMBERS    MARCH 28, 1997

*To Kyum Hwan, Jang Hwan, and Jin Won*

I want to talk with all of you for a long while, but because of limited time, I am going to give my regards through this letter. Kyum Hwan! Jang Hwan! Jin Won! I can give a brief description of the spirit world, which you cannot see, like this:

"What a useless life the physical world was!
It was nothing.
It was nothing.
Oh! God!
Oh! God!"

I don't really know how I can describe this infinite spirit world. God is invisible. Even though I am in the kingdom of heaven, I cannot see God. However, there is brilliant and fascinating light, which cannot be explained by the human brain, intellect, and reason. Before such a bright light, all the contents of our lives are disclosed completely. In this brilliant light, we can have the same feeling of relief, safety, and happiness as a baby feels when it is drinking its mother's milk. In this light, everything seems to be melted like a blast furnace. We can call it the blast furnace of God's love. Oh God! Such a wonderful world lies ahead! A sweet scent, a beautiful melody, such as we have never experienced.

My children! Even if your father tried to write all night about the spirit world, I would not be able to adequately express myself. Let me ask a question. How much longer are you going to live on earth? What is the purpose of your lives? As your parent, I want to ask you to read thoroughly Unification Thought, which I wrote, and the Divine Principle, which True Father wrote. After reading that, you should decide your way of life. If there is a greater teaching than those books, you may follow that. However, if you think that there is no such greater thought, you should work with your whole energy and life for the sake of God's will. You should not listen to the local news regarding various bad rumors and negative things about the Unification Church, but you ought to listen to the national news.

On the day of the Seung Hwa ceremony, many people over-praised me. I want you as my children to receive those expressions humbly. In the near future, I will explain about this huge spirit world through Mrs. Kim, after organizing my thinking systematically and logically. I will also speak to the group of professors about the spirit world. You also have to help Mrs. Kim. You should study how to live. Please keep in mind that the physical world in which you are living is a valueless and momentary world.

—From your father

*To My Beloved Sons (A letter from Your Mother.)*

Kyum Hwan! Jang Hwan! Jin Won! Please listen 100 percent to what your father said. As your mother, what I want to ask to you is that you have close relationships with one another and help others. Please always look around to see if there is anything with which you can help. How are you going to manage the problem of inheritance? After discussing that matter among yourselves, please talk to Mrs. Kim. Your father said that he would then finalize that. I also ask that you study the True Parents. How happy you are because you can listen to this precious news from the spirit world! As your mother, I deeply appreciate that.

—From your mother

*After Examining My Life, Please Study Unification Thought*

After examining my life, please study Unification Thought. Please, follow me. (A father's advice to his sons.)

*Questions and Answers with Family Members*

Q: What do you think of impiety?

A: Since I did not completely fulfill my duty of filial piety before God, how can I ask for the filial piety of my sons? If you want to perform the duty of filial piety, please follow True Parents.

Q: Why did you go through the window?

A: Nobody would go through a window if one knew that it was a window. But I went through the window because it looked like an open exit. Please, don't ask me any more about that. I have no regret about my past life. I do not even repent. If there is something about which I need to repent, it is that I was not much more intellectually enlightened. [Ed.: Dr. Lee's death was preceded by an accident in which he fell through a window.]

Q: What shall we do with your belongings?

A: Please donate any important things to Sun Moon University and burn the rest.

Instruction to his sons: You should live for the sake of God's will. If you think that Unification Thought and Divine Principle are truth, you should follow that with all your mind, heart, and life. What will be necessary for you to do? Practice the truth after judging what is helpful to God's will! In the spirit world, I will develop educational materials that can be of vital assistance to people in the physical world.

## Instruction to Staff of the Unification Thought Institute

Please develop the the Unification Thought Institute. I will help you.

## God's Words

(1) Sang Hun Lee! Congratulations on your arrival into God's bosom!

(2) God called me a "Heavenly Man."

(3) God said that Sang Hun tries to circulate throughout the spirit world and physical world, and that he is working very hard.

## Private Conversation

Mrs. Kim! I hope that you can come here after living on earth for the same time as me. Through you, I want to disclose everything about the spirit world as far as I am able. We now can join together in new marriage. (Mrs. Kim saw a vision in which family members were gathering around the dining table of their house filled with brilliant light.)

*To Churl Ha Hwang and Jong Sam Lee*

"Thank you for attending today's meeting. Please publish this letter as a well-developed book to deliver to intellectual groups." ( 10 PM, July 21, 1997)

## THE SPIRIT WORLD AND ITS LIFE   *MAY 23, 1997*

Mrs. Kim! My name is Sang Hun Lee. When you test me to see if I am a Satan, you offend me. I would appreciate it very much if you would believe me when God introduces me.

*Spirit World*

Even though the spirit world appears to be the same as the visible phenomenal world, the scale of the spirit world cannot be compared with the scale of the physical world. For instance, in the phenomenal world, materiality and space limit a car, but in the spirit world, a car's form can be changed at will. Its direction of movement is also free. The car moves with a driver's thought and can even pass through a mountain in a moment. It can move as freely as in fantasy movies or science fiction travel, which children like very much. Even though the motion of the car may look chaotic, because they are keeping spiritual law, there are no accidents at all.

## Life in the Spirit World

Earthly people wake up in the morning and sleep at night, and spirit persons behave the same way. However, in the spirit world, morning and night do not follow a regular order. Morning and night can be changed according to one's thinking.

I do not know who first described the spirit world as containing hell, Paradise, and the kingdom of heaven respectively, but the distinctions are proper. Huge gaps exist in these levels of life. For one thing, hell is very bizarre. We can never see comparable sights in the physical world.

For instance, I saw one woman standing nude, and beside her, a man touched the lower part of her body. Beside them, another woman fought with her, arguing that the man's lower part was her own. Despite their grotesque nature, they did not feel ashamed.

Once, when a Japanese woman ran wearing wooden shoes and fell down, another woman came and hid the shoes as if they were her own. The woman who lost her shoes then tried to find them, while the woman who hid the shoes feigned ignorance. Then, others who saw all that had occurred shouted out that the woman was a thief, and attacked her, striking and kicking. These things happen very often.

When an old man cannot eat food because he injured his finger, a young man comes and takes the elder's food, stuffing it into his mouth. These things always happen in hell. Another woman, who was forced to cut off her hair, felt ashamed, and hid her head with a towel. But people passing by her, took her towel and cleaned their hands and faces with it. When the owner of the towel took it again from the people and covered her head, people forcibly grabbed it back, cut it in half with scissors and returned the other half to her. Then, because she could not hide her shame, she withdrew to a dark place.

## ORIGINAL HEAVEN AND HELL IN
## THE SPIRIT WORLD                    JUNE 1, 1997

*(Today's words were spoken not with excitement but with quiet and calm.)*

### Heaven Is the Place Where Thought and Action Become One

What kind of name is heaven? I don't know, but these sentences are written either in heaven or Eden. No matter, it is the place where words and deeds are one.

As an example, if I think, "Today what kind of meat will I eat, what do I want to eat?" with that thought simultaneously a huge feast will appear before me. Also, if I think, "Today where do I want to go, who do I want to see?" I'm already there. Even if I think, "What if that person isn't dressed when I arrive there?" and he happens to be stark naked, then we will have a good laugh.

Recently I thought, "When blind people come to heaven, will they be different from those who had sight on earth?" A grandfather and a midget suddenly stood in front of me. The midget had been blind, but the grandfather had possessed good eyesight, so I asked, "In heaven, are there blind people?" Their answer was, "We came because you asked a question. While on earth I was blind, but here in heaven there is not even the term, blindness; there is no blindness. I can see everything." I asked, "Grandfather, you can see, so why did you come?" He said, "You asked about the difference between a person who had earthly sight and one who had not. You can see both with your eyes and with your mind. With eyes you can visibly see an object, but the thing you can see with your mind you can see better than with your eyes."

16

In heaven, the environment abounds with many bright jewels. Because of the surrounding brightness and luster, you cannot hide any difficulties between each other. Everything can be seen and known with the eyes and mind. If I am filled with light and my hair dazzles golden, it is due to a golden light that is filled with a radiant ecstasy. This is the place where your mind is always filled with peace and serenity, where difficulty, discomfort and hunger do not exist. Heaven is the place where you will find no difficulty to express or explain anything.

### Hell Is the Place You Cannot Imagine in Heaven

In hell you endure hunger and suffering; hell swims in jealousy and discomfort. Due to such suffering, fighting cannot be avoided. Everyone feels uncomfortable. In heaven you have the freedom to follow your mind, but in hell you can't do a single thing according to your own will. In hell, you take others' possessions by force and eat by stealth. People on earth cannot imagine how bad hell really is.

### "Sang Hun Ah!" This Is Love

[Ed.: Only his parents, grandparents or close friends would refer to Dr. Sang Hun Lee as "Sang Hun ah."]

On earth, if Father introduces a story of love, He always speaks in reference to convex and concave. When you think of love you think about convex and concave, but these words, you realize, are too technical.

Calling out, "Sang-Hun-ah," that sound has such a feeling of love that it melts down everything. Love possesses such sensitivity that it must forgive even a brutal crime, or be comfortable when near a person who stinks with the smell of old fish. Even then love possesses the passive feeling of ease and comfort. The word "love" does not adequately describe the heart. Something more is needed. It's having a feeling totally without envy. Even in the most normal circumstances, when you take a step, or speak a word, or when you wear clothes, using just the word, "love," is unsatisfactory. For God, there is no phrase beautiful or deep enough to express or encompass the thought of love. God calls out, "Sang-Hun-ah! That's love!" If you flawlessly embrace the will of love, there will be no fighting or suffering on earth. There is no adequate way to elucidate perfectly the word "love." This is love.

## The Concept of Heaven and Hell

In heaven there is no way to worry or have any anxiety at all. You are living and going about as one mass of love perfectly suited. Hell is the place where you spin around on the edge of discomfort, worry, anxiety and conflict, because you live in a world where you cannot know anything about love. In summation, hell is the place alienated from love, and heaven is the holy, perfect unity of love. Simply speaking, heaven is the place where there is nothing that doesn't have love, and hell is the place where there is not one iota of love. It is possible for the fruit of love to bud and sprout and bring about the liberation of hell.

## THE MIDDLE REALMS
## OF SPIRIT WORLD          JUNE 1-JULY 28, 1997

*What Is the Middle Realm of Spirit World?*

On the earth, what we thought of as the middle realm of Spirit World is actually somewhat different. Amidst the many communities of the world, people worked to establish nations that are far away from service to God. People work to elevate themselves without concern for religion; they gather in places without a relationship of faith.

In this place it is difficult to see something which resembles either heaven or hell. There are many similarities to the earth. As an example, during mealtime in the kitchen, someone is working, someone is cleaning dishes, preparing food, or serving food; everyone will work together. To describe the people in this realm: in heaven people are very bright; in hell, people are always uneasy and restless, but here people are always very busy and working hard, never resting. At a special event, people will be alive with energy, but there is no concern whatsoever for God or religion.

In this place people hear the Unification Thought lecture, but some people ask foolish questions, such as, isn't there a world where only people alike live together? Their questions make no sense or are extremely simplistic. You feel that witnessing will take a very long time. The middle realm of Spirit World is not heaven and not hell, but has many different levels. It's a place where it is very difficult to get across to people any idea of God or Principle or Unification Thought.

The middle realms are massive, so the variety is difficult to explain. In this realm the common people are very distinguishable from Unification members. Unification members are full of life. You can't observe any difficulty among them. Also they are filled with peace and they live enthusiastically. If they have some workshop, there is a lot of fun and games and laughter and enjoyment. Compared to our members, others appear very different. They have no pulse, no life. Their activities are very passive and lazy. They have weary and tired faces. Why do the common people, as opposed to Unification Church members, have such a sad demeanor? It's because they have no hope and no desire. But Unification Church members in the middle realms have hope and desire because they expect and wait for God's special privilege to come to them and they know God's basic will. Common people don't know God's will. They are not in a place of hope. The common people and Unification Church members stay in different regions.

Sadly, there are many members who cannot stay in the Unification realm of spirit world. There are many reasons for this. First, even though a couple received the Blessing, one person deviated from the path and they could not establish a family. Or second, they received the Blessing, but the couple lived without care for God's will. Or third, the couple received the Blessing but their life became uncentered. There are many cases like this. They have the form and name of Unification member. Since they are called members, they may come to the middle region of spirit world.

What do they do in this place? This group of members always dwells in the place where they can receive God's, Heung Jin Nim's, and True Parents' special Blessings and favor. How? They can enjoy time together, listen to Divine Principle lectures and receive faith guidance. Therefore they all have hope. Also, this area receives a lot of attention from God and Heung Jin Nim.

People of the world can enter this middle region of Spirit World, but only Unification Church members can enter a special classroom to receive education regarding the direction of righteousness and justice. This is really amazing. You don't understand the meaning of the Blessing while on earth, because you can't see it. But from heaven there is an exorbitant condition that can be received. True Parents are giving the Blessing without price. The reason is because of our Parents' merit. While True Parents are living on the earth in this time, they are giving great Blessings to you. So we must go out to give the Blessing to many people in our area. That is the Unification way of giving Blessing to others.

*Paradise*

Paradise on earth was thought to be somewhere between heaven and hell, but that is not accurate. In Paradise people form groups within which they naturally belong. For example, Koreans go to Korea town, Chinese go to Chinatown, and Japanese go to Japan town.

## LIFE ON EARTH VIEWED
## FROM SPIRIT WORLD                        JUNE 9, 1997

*How Are Works People Do on Earth*
*Recorded in Spirit World?*

How people live life on earth determines what is recorded in Spirit World. For example, how a president of a country lived his life is recorded in Spirit World. Whether or not he lived his life for himself or for the sake of his country is what is officially recorded. If your life was just spent on petty things or you were irrationally materialistic, or if you were simply an evil person, not a true person, it is all recorded. It is just as if you were to write your own autobiography. As you arrange the final moments of your life, you will consider how you established your life's path. God appears unconditionally. How wonderful if in your life you worked hard. Even the president of a country comes to Spirit World without pretense. The foundation of your life will appear in front of you.

You become a complete spirit person 40 days after your life ends. During this 40 days you travel back and forth between the physical and spirit worlds, and your place of residence is prepared. During this time God does not intervene. Although your ancestors will cooperate with you, they cannot help you 100 percent. You have to work yourself to establish your residence. No one judges you. Each person's seat of judgment is different. After you go to your home, if you get set up in the place where you desire as far as geography and topography are concerned, no one will force something upon you. Your spirit guide will appear and naturally direct you.

According to the way of Spirit World, the atmosphere of guidance or judgement is different. You may receive some benefit as a result of having spent time as the president of a country, although there were conditions in place that allowed you to make a large contribution to the nation. There is no room for not keeping a position of goodness; if you don't keep your existence of value, then you'll receive punishment up to and not more than you justly deserve. This is the spirit world. Whether you were the president or a person at the opposite end of the social spectrum, class distinction holds no sway over the spiritual foundation.

We estimate the value of a person from a moral basis, and ask to what extent he lived a righteous life. "In spirit world," a medium asked, "isn't there an awareness of social distinction between the lowest level worker and those with scholarly achievement? In the physical world there exists such a distinction between the learned and the unlearned." Dr. Lee answered: "In spirit world, the field of your work is different from your scholarly major on earth. But your greatest embarrassment is not that, but comes rather if you made a mistake in your life and you were ignorant of the value of your life. The manner in which the distinction of academic achievement appears in Spirit World differs from the way it appears on earth."

*The Difference Between*
*Religious and Non-Religious People*

The difference between a person of faith and a person of no faith is enormous. This creates a considerable class structure, or several levels. While living a life of faith, a sincere person may be able to draw close to God's favor. However, even if you live according to faith, if you lack conscientiousness, your faith doesn't matter. Such a person will reside in a position similar to one who lived in ignorance of God, in a place where God has nothing to do with them. Regarding religious and non-religious people, God's grace comes later to the non-religious. Even in heaven, when a favor is bestowed, apprehensions arise. God gives His blessing to humankind through the Holy Spirit. Through loving humankind, heaven also receives benefit. The time will come when in freedom you will move to a place you desire, one that reflects the spiritual merit you achieved while in your body. At that time, you will move based on God's command.

*What Is the Difference Between Unification Members' Position and Other Religions' Members?*

A huge difference exists. I can explain this in a word. In spirit world, regions differ. Here, according to the former life of each member, each one differs a little from another, but all the various realms in Spirit World are significantly different. Here, the thing that is hugely different is the position in relation to God.

Limits exist which determine how well people belonging to another religion can hear, feel or talk to God. But Unification Church members by all means reside in a position where they may breathe together with God. Among Unification Church members, there exist several layers. There are distinguishable, revered positions. I'm sorry, but it is for the sake of our members that Sang Hun Lee is speaking, to enable and help us to adjust our lives here on earth and to assist us when we go to Spirit World. Differences arise according to how we went the way of True Parents. The position of the 36 couples is most intense. This is the highest family position, but I cannot easily express all the difficulty and hardship connected with it. Particularly, we have all of our mistakes disclosed.

When on earth, many members or their families get caught in the problem of women, the problem of public money, or other similar problems. Eventually, we all go to live in God's house and there, everything of one's self is exposed. For example, we see at all times someone's sin of having sex with a different woman. We can see in detail the sins of a man who used public money for himself and went to a bar and fell with a woman. The Unification Church members reside in a place more frightening than hell. The same holds true for a low-level family or any other type of family.

Many levels exist according to the nature of the crime or sin committed. However, we mostly reside in the realm of Spirit World closest to God. We also maintain a prison where people with grave sins must stay. How wonderful it is we can go the way of indemnifying our sin by gathering in such a place among those criminals. No place exists where one can indemnify and solve sin alone. Through prayer, tithing, service and other such public efforts made by their descendants on earth, the door to the prison will be opened for spirit persons and they will be able to leave. When such persons leave prison, they will receive spiritual guidance according to their position.

After paying all our indemnity, at that point will we be able to live peacefully? Yes, once our descendants indemnify our sin. So if our descendants pray for us and offer their whole heart, the spirits which benefit from that indemnity will escape their misery. But our position is to escape only to return again. If earthly people pray and invest their heart, it inevitably shortens a person's indemnity period. However, on earth they mostly don't know a person's situation. So many must undergo a course of mental suffering for quite a long time.

If one's path of hardship is long in Spirit World, then whether the descendants on earth know it or not, he will be incessantly hindered. If ancestors suffer, their descendants also must endure in an uncomfortable position. More simply put, when ancestors commit crime, descendants receive punishment. There is no other path but to remember the way of heaven. Each must go the way of righteousness.

# LIFE ON EARTH
# AND SPIRIT PEOPLE                      JUNE 16, 1997

Mrs. Kim! This is Sang Hun Lee. I am Sang Hun Lee. If you record my words, your health will gradually improve.

## Life in Spirit World

Spirit people decide their own position by how they lived on earth. If you lived selfishly, then you will suffer in a position praying for a thousand years without special grace. People in the Spirit World who lived in peace on earth also enable their descendants to live peacefully. But if people lived evil lives, then when they come to Spirit World, they live in hell and their descendants are always oppressed with problems. For example: If we examine a person who suffers hell in the Spirit World, they really exist in pain.

The environment is dark, and as in a prison, there is no freedom. There is nothing to eat or wear. Your descendants on earth can do nothing to undo and disentangle all your evil deeds. They do not know how to carry your burden or how to pray for you. But, if their ancestors' wrongdoing becomes known, and the descendants serve with utmost sincerity and prayer, then the spirit person can receive grace. That spirit person can move to a better place where he is treated hospitably and undergoes a change. Who will make that happen? That is the subject of my talk today. Whether you spend money on earth or not, there exists some support for you, but it's not the same in Spirit World. The wind blows, flowers bloom and birds sing but you can't change just because someone commands you to. There is no one whose mere command can change you. The resolution to change can only happen within you. You must reach the point of self-awareness.

If descendants sincerely offer their hearts for the sinners in Spirit World, then such spirit people can come to the point of understanding themselves and how they must change. Fortunately, there are many people who understand this spiritual law. On earth, when a shaman dances and delves into the ancestors' situation, they can only comfort the ancestors. The shaman cannot solve their ancestors' problems. But if the ancestors receive grace through the sincere and elevated prayer of their descendants, then they may be able to search out heaven's messenger and God's commandment.

### The Life of Earthly People

Therefore, people's lives on earth are very important. It takes too much time to improve your position as a spirit person so you can receive effective grace. It takes a long time to move beyond ignorance. Because of that, adjust your focus now on the eternal world and live that way. Through adjusting your focus, humankind will live much more wisely. We hope no person will be foolish in their faith and make eternal mistakes because the natural consequence is a nation full of foolish people here. They can't solve anything. Regarding life in that country, I can't explain everything, but, to summarize it in a word, your life should be fruitful; you should bear fruit. To speak more plainly: committing sin leads only to hell. Live a life of goodness. That is the way of heaven. Please live well for the sake of eternity.

# EARTHLY PEOPLE AND SPIRIT PERSONS HAVE A DIFFERENT VIEWPOINT JUNE 23, 1997

Mrs. Kim! This is Sang Hun Lee. Thank you. Thank you very much for preparing your mind beforehand to receive.

## Earthly People

First, let's take a look at the people on earth. Earthly people look with physical eyes, touch physically and act physically. Earthly people live physically limited to a confined amount of space. For example: Human beings live through a time period of 10, 20, or 60 years. Also, on earth, though I desired an object, I could not automatically obtain it. Earth people may artificially make things, but they cannot adequately bring into existence something in the mind that occurred as thought. Earth people get hungry, but if they don't move they won't eat. Also, because you act within finite space, when someone misses you in the realm of thought, it just stops there. Also, when you go through physical pain, you don't know the solution as a certainty. For example, when people of faith have an illness, they will turn to prayer and other such approaches to healing, but non-believers just go to the hospital.

## Spirit People

Spirit people are different. Spirit people, because the physical body does not confine them, have an infinite realm in which to act. Let's look at an example: whether looking, touching or acting, because it appears immediately with your thought, there is no length of time. Because spirit people can simultaneously move something with thought, just as with the touch of the hand, time is condensed and it doesn't require someone else to aid you to solve a problem. At the same instant a spirit person thinks, another spirit person can receive it, and this doesn't require words. When a spirit person develops his logic with definitiveness and exact precision, he can transmit the exact details and they will appear right before the face of the other person. So you can very quickly express your circumstances because your partner immediately recognizes your expression of feeling.

Spirit people can know completely all of God's creation process from the beginning, as well as the whole concept of what we call a person, so we can never cause God pain. (This is one thing that separates heaven from hell.) Spirit people, if they work hard in their own sphere, will evolve as the highest master of a skill and will receive their reward. Thus, no greed exists and they always carry a tranquil countenance. (This is also a dividing point of heaven and hell.) In other words, for the sake of solving a problem of food or clothing, there arises no harassment or annoyance, and our facial expressions remain benign and humble. If I summarize the difference between physical and spirit people, physical people live and act within the confines of space. They remain busy acting to solve difficult problems and they suffer due to food and clothing needs, but spirit people can move freely throughout limitless space. Because the worries of food and clothing have been removed, we are infinitely bright and humble. Our conclusion: bear good fruit in your physical life and when you come to heaven you will appreciate the correctness of this teaching.

## The Principle of Duality in Spirit World

In the Divine Principle, in the discourse on Unification Thought, the principle of duality teaches that give and take action takes place when subject and object give and receive, reciprocally generating Origin-Division-Union Action (O-D-U Action). Through this we receive joy. This is the fundamental principle of God. So let's talk about the difference between the physical and spirit worlds. In the physical realm, when subject and object, through give and take action, achieve O-D-U Action, there is joy at becoming one. In Spirit World, the feeling of joy that comes from becoming one in O-D-U Action through give and take action is somewhat different. For example: In the process of giving to another and their reception, there is no time involved. Because O-D-U happens with thought, you don't actually see any sign of give and take action. This is a clearly revealed account of the basis for heaven, where completed individuals are gathered according to the principle of duality.

## Give and Take Action in Spirit World

The fundamental concept of give and take action is unity between subject and object through giving and receiving with each other and becoming one through love. We can see this achieves the model of the kingdom of heaven. In heaven, give and take action happens even when you just look up towards each other; you become literally one perfect body. But in hell, or outside of this realm, there exists a lot of difference in the level of give and take action based on the class or position of each person. The fundamental teaching of the Creation Principle is that give and take action in heaven is where you fundamentally accomplish and complete the purpose of God's creation. Because hell is the place where you cannot understand God's foundation at all, there exists only one relative principle in hell. Even as you progress, you must think of one very important point in order to achieve the liberation of hell: You must strive towards the goal of give and take action. This is very similar to the situation on earth.

### The Intimate Relationship between Life on Earth and Life in Heaven

How can my life on Earth be consummated in heaven? The eternal position in which we are placed is decided based on the standard of good or evil during our life on earth. Based on whom my life was centered upon on earth, my position in the eternal world (God's side, Satan's side, atheist) is decided. Though there might be some differences based on individual achievement, a spirit of nationalism and a worldview, the formation of personality is far more important in heaven than is a spirit of nationalism or a worldview. The thought that because I worked in a higher position on earth, I will be placed in a higher position in heaven, is wrong. Therefore, the most worthwhile and fruitful way is to live with my heart centered on God, renouncing personal greed and leading a life of reverence and respect. Then we can live with our heads up in heaven.

### Questions and Answers

Questions from Dr. Lee's daughter

Q: What should we do to compensate for our impiety in not attending you in your lifetime?

A: I just want to ask you to live sincerely and faithfully in your position.

Q: Please give a word of direction to your children.

A: I do not want to engage in clumsy explanation. If you think the path your parents have followed is correct, just follow the path. Yet, if you think otherwise, then there is nothing I can do about it. I will think that your father's life was not enough for you.

Q: What about the books we are keeping?

A: Donate them to Sun Moon University (Institute of Research for Unification Ideology).

Q: What about the problem of the burial ground?

A: Just do as you please. I have done nothing good for God, have I ?

The property...?

A: I want you to do as you please.

*Inseung's Questions*
*(Dr. Lee's Son)*

Q: In heaven is there a difference between the face of a Miss Korea and a homely face?

A: Those pretty faces on earth are still pretty here. However, those homely faces are endlessly beautiful because a beautiful heart is expressed through them and they radiate the light of God. Pretty faces in hell cannot be compared with even homely faces in heaven. Though our faces do not change their shape (a round face remains round and a long face long), since the true beauty of the face is determined based on how we lead our lives on earth, those who are trying to come to heaven by cultivating their hearts and characters are indeed wise.

Q: How great a difference exists between those who are courageous and those who are cowardly?

A: Courage and cowardice are not that important to God. Try your best on earth to come to heaven since the desire for heaven does not come from courage, nor are people ignored because they are cowards.

*Question from the Medium*
*(Y.S. Kim)*

Q: Are you reading from your notes or just speaking as you think?
A: It is very complicated and hard to explain. Whenever I think, it just appears to me as recorded. It can be said that your thoughts are automatically recorded.

## THE FUNDAMENTAL MEANING OF LOVE

Mrs. Kim! To describe the scene here for a moment: the present time is very precious. Many people who received direction from God are praying and are about to begin their work. Now, let us begin. Love, as the letter can explain, is the state of mind where you are acting with all your heart, sincerely and devotedly for others. In love, there exist conjugal love, spiritual love, and religious agape love.

*Conjugal Love*

Conjugal love is the love where men and women are connected physically. On earth, we can feel emotion when our bodies can meet and love. But in heaven, a man and woman without physical bodies can love. The conjugal love between those high spirits (those who are close to God) is like a beautiful picture. Since the bodies of the two become totally one when they love, they can feel a strong emotion through their bodies and minds which goes beyond the feeling of love they felt on Earth. It is like creating a higher existence from the state of a complete absence of ego. It is like feeling you are in a magical world.

Also, you can actually view the scene of making love with your own eyes. Couples on Earth make love in their bedrooms most of the time. Here, in heaven, that is absolutely not the case. It is not a hidden love, which you can only perform in your bedroom. In heaven, you might love among wild flowers in a field, on beautiful land or on an ocean wave. You can even love in the mountains where the birds are singing and the scene is so beautiful that those who watch you will become intoxicated. Rather than feeling shame or disgrace as you felt on the earth, you can observe the scene with a peaceful mind, admiring the beauty.

Hell is just the opposite. People in hell make love hidden away, and those who see the conjugal scene curse them. They point their fingers at them saying they are ugly. Those love scenes in hell are very similar to those on Earth.

## Spiritual Love

Since spiritual love is not physically observed through the action of the body, it looks to some as though it is not related to those who live on the Earth. Yet, it is a love that is absolutely necessary to those who live on the Earth. Since everybody has his or her own inner self, if you do not cultivate your inner self well, you are going to encounter many problems in making your love complete (becoming one as husband and wife) in heaven.

For example, suppose there is one couple where the husband's inner self is well cultivated while the inner self of the wife is not; then there will not be complete love in this family. Then what will happen? They cannot make an elegant and beautiful love. Yet since they have a desire to love, they will make conjugal love with only limited love, in limited places, such as their bedroom.

Then how can these couples make a complete love? When the husband's heart to respect his wife and the wife's heart to love her husband become one, their love can develop and mature into a complete love. Since this takes a longer time to achieve in heaven, when you are on Earth, with your own physical body, you have to try to cultivate your heart and bear the fruit of complete love.

In conclusion, we should use our short life on Earth well, in anticipation of the complete love that will be awaiting the mature couple in heaven. Couples bear the fruit of complete love by cultivating and encouraging each other to achieve true love.

## Agape Love Due to Religion

When God created us, He bestowed on us the capacity for unconditional love. This is Agape Love. However, due to the Human Fall and the subsequent changes over the ages, the original standard of love God gave to us has been deteriorating. Therefore, because of the resulting existence of hell, God and human beings endured much pain in their hearts. In reverse, by acknowledging the worth of unconditional, fundamental love, the path to the liberation of hell can be opened up and hell can be destroyed. Conjugal Love and Spiritual Love must exist only between husband and wife. However, by the destruction of this kind of relationship of love, humanity became separated from their foundation of God's unconditional love. God wanted to endlessly bestow Love upon us. With this love you want to give and give, and it becomes bigger and bigger even after you give.

However, since the foundation was destroyed, today, the road to salvation has become difficult. By establishing the true sense of husband and wife, we must love, trust and have a conciliatory attitude toward each other. Sometimes, we must forgive and reconcile with each other.

Therefore, by becoming one with the love God bestowed upon us, the road to the liberation of all humankind will be opened and hell in the eternal world will disappear. Accordingly, if we trust and love each other, neither hell nor war will afflict humankind. Because we led our lives without knowing this principle well, the way to the heavenly world became complicated, and the groaning punishment of hell came into being. We must cultivate and keep a strong love between husband and wife, and cultivate the fundamental inborn love God bestowed to us.

## THE ACTIVITY OF SPIRIT SELVES THROUGH PERSONS ON EARTH

### Spirit Selves' Help for Persons on Earth

The spirits in the Spirit World cannot improve themselves without the cooperation of persons on Earth. That is, our spirit selves were created to live forever in the Spirit World based upon the foundation of life on the Earth. Therefore, unless spirit selves can rid themselves of the sins they committed, they are destined to live receiving punishment, forever. For example, when a murderer comes to the Spirit World, a horrible (cruel) punishment will be with him forever. He who killed a man with a knife, his spirit self will be stabbed with a knife; he who shot a man to death, his spirit self will have a bullet stuck in his heart.

Also, he who beat a man to death with a stone, his spirit self has to live with his eyes pulled out, and his body being bruised and bloody. He who killed a person by kicking with his feet, his spirit self will stay prostrated with his face down while being stepped on with his own feet. He who killed a person with poison, his spirit self will be collapsed spitting blood, and he who killed a man with an ax or sickle will have the instrument stuck in the chest of his spirit self.

Among those spirit selves, some try to hide the sins they committed on earth, yet they cannot be hidden despite their efforts. Those spirit selves also try to liquidate their past sins on Earth, yet it cannot be done as they wish. Myriad spirits are trying hard to lead a life better than their current situations; again, it cannot be accomplished as they wish. Those spirit selves miss life on Earth and are willing to do any odd and peculiar things to rid themselves of their sins. However, the record once entered cannot be erased. It is common for all spirit selves that they wish to hide and erase their lives on Earth (the sinful behaviors), and feel shameful of those lives being shown to others, yet it seems more tragic since their efforts to hide and erase are also shown to others so vividly.

## How Do Spirit Selves Help Persons on Earth?

In order for the spirit selves to be liberated from their positions, they cannot avoid pain and suffering without the help of the people on Earth. Also, since they cannot rid themselves of the sins they committed, the spirit selves definitely go to the place (they lived on Earth). They go to their own blood and flesh, or someone related in some way, and keep sending signals. However, because those who live on Earth are not aware of it, unusual disasters happen, such as a sick person at home, financial difficulties, or automobile accidents. Finally, when the descendent can find out the reason, and therefore can pray and donate for that spirit self, then the spirit self can be promoted to a little bit better position (from his current position) in recognition of his descendant's services. However, if they do not know the reason, then there will be continuous accidents and mishaps, and people will die. As a result, there will be more troubled ancestors. Therefore, if a family cannot find any problems in their faith, but nevertheless has continuous accidents big or small, it can be concluded that this family has ancestors who have complicated problems. Then the fastest way to solve these problems is through prayer, with faith.

Now, the fortune-teller, whose spiritual level is rather low, can solve the issue, yet those spirit selves can only be consoled temporarily; their suffering and pain cannot be solved completely. This is the big difference between those who know God and those who do not. (The spirit selves can stay for quite a while, yet, as time passes, they will be the same.) The spirit selves do not have any solutions from where they are placed, despite their struggling and wiggling at their position. The more severe those spirit selves' lives become, the more difficult and complicated the lives of their descendent on Earth become. The spirit selves in the Spirit World, in order to receive the cooperation from those on Earth, come to their descendants mobilizing all sorts of methods. However, because the descendants do not know the method to solve the problem, the family's fortune will wane and the ancestors' painful lives will repeat themselves. Since those spirit selves who advanced to better positions with the help of the people on Earth can lead more comfortable lives, the lives of their descendent can be more peaceful.

*The Relationship between Spirit Selves*
*and Persons on Earth*

Now, let's examine the relationship between the people on Earth and the spirit self in the Spirit World. The relationship between those two can be compared with that between needle and thread. That is, the relationship between the people on Earth and the spirit self in the Spirit World is like the relationship between the body and spirit. Also the relationship between the two is like the one between husband and wife who cannot be separated and therefore become one. Therefore, it goes without saying that the person on Earth should lead a good life when they have a physical body. However, it is when they no longer have a body, that is, when they already become spirit selves, they come to a realization that they did not lead a good life. I would like to conclude that when you live on Earth with your body, you have to prepare for the eternal life, summarize your life, and lead everyday life sincerely and faithfully.

What and how can the descendants do for the sake of those spirit selves who already lost their bodies? Their position can be comfortable when the descendent on Earth prays for them. Today, the status that our True Parents granted us, the right to become a Tribal Messiah, is an immensely special status. It is great that I can save my ancestors through prayer in my name. Therefore, because my life on Earth can be made comfortable by praying for my ancestors, thereby having them ascend to more comfortable places, it is natural that I should save my ancestors. Keeping in mind that this is the path by which we can offer a little help to our True Parents, by easing the pain of our True Parents in the Spirit World, we have to complete our lives when we have our own bodies on Earth well.

It is so natural that we have to complete our duties as Tribal

Messiahs for our ancestors' favor, and it also can become the path for those spirit selves who observed it, to receive a special grant.

The medium asked, "In the relationship between the person on Earth and the Spirit Self in the Spirit World, do those spirit selves who are placed in good positions without any difficulties still need cooperation, favor, or prayer from the person on Earth?" And his answer is as follows, "Since a human is composed of spirit and body, a dual structure, the principle is that those who lost their bodies should live in the Spirit World and those who have bodies are supposed to live on Earth.

"It should be assumed that there must be reasons the spirit selves send signals to the person on Earth. Because of the tie of the blood lineage, they are sending signals, sometimes for good purposes and sometimes for bad. The person on Earth should be able to discriminate between these based on the Law of Principle, and the spirit self should not confuse the person on Earth. Many times, since God does not intervene in the matter of blood lineage, we human beings should find rebirth through the spirit of God in order to live truthful lives."

*Common Point of Spirit Selves and Persons on Earth*

Since the people on Earth have bodies, there are times when they cannot do whatever they wish at their convenience. The spirit selves, though, do not have a body and are free to move within their position (through different degrees of freedom obtained based on the position). The person on Earth, though, has a body and leads a limited life everywhere. Spirit selves, though, without a body, can lead an active life in the eternal world. The person on Earth, though, has a body and cannot occupy an eternal place. Spirit selves do not have a body, so they can have an eternal place. If I list the differences between those two, it will be endless.

Now, let's examine the points they share in common. Both life on Earth and life in the Spirit World are only half the story. Therefore each can accomplish only half. Then, how can the successful resolution of body and mind lead to the bearing of complete fruit? Before the body and spirit are separated by physical death, they have to finish their lives on Earth. Then they can be complete fruit. However, when the spirit person comes to Spirit World with their spirits not fully ripe, there arise problems. Therefore, to solve the problems, the relationship between the ancestors and the descendent becomes complicated.

Now, again, we have to bear in mind the importance of life lived on Earth. In order to live forever in the beautiful house God prepared for us, we should not live for the "half life" as our goal. I hope your life on Earth is the one that can bear the complete fruit of spirit and body and therefore greet the harvest season with joy.

While recording the message, the medium showed some doubts about Dr. Sang Hun Lee. Then he said, "Please let's stop writing the phrase, 'I am Sang Hun Lee who wrote the Unification ideology.'"

## THE IMAGE OF GOD'S LOVE          JUNE 14, 1997

*I, Sang Hun Lee*

I, Sang Hun Lee, came to the Spirit World from Earth. My only purpose is to graft the ideology of the True Parents into others. This is because I came to realize that there is no ideology higher than that of the True Parents.

### True Love and False Love

Love is a precious element God gives human beings when they are born. But the heartbreaking situation is that it was this very love that led to the reality of men and women serving two owners even from birth. This is the beginning of our misfortune. Human beings cannot truly live on the physical love between husband and wife alone. Love is the most precious constituent of personality endowed to us. Due to the human Fall, we lost the essence of love. Original love was overlaid with fallen and ugly love, so love manifests as artificial love. Love is located at the very center of God's nature. We cannot fully analyze nor disclose this love within God. Nonetheless, I am going to report on this fundamental love in the Spirit World.

### God's Love

God's love cannot be touched or expressed, nor can we verify God's love with our eyes. God's love is hard to understand. Also, the human brain cannot analyze God's love. God's love, though given to us endlessly, is never diminished. As when a water tap is left open, God's love springs forth continuously. Though we receive and receive God's love, we never dislike it nor can we ever have too much of it. On the contrary, the more we receive the more we become humble as we beg for more.

Though God's love cannot be measured by weight or bulk, it has infinite value for us. I would like to speak of God's love as follows. Suppose that the whole world received God's love simultaneously and returned all the love to God. Even if this took place, God would still have more love. Then how can the measure of God's love toward human beings be expressed? God can neither be seen nor touched. God is neither limited material nor a solid mass. Then, how can human beings express God's love, and how can human beings realize God's love?

I am going to analyze "God who loves Sang Hun Lee." Let's do it.

God calls me, "Sang Hun." I hear the voice clearly with my own ears. Then a brilliant, glittering, radiating and reflecting light appears in front of, behind and above my head. Amid the light, a streak of light, unidentified, captures my heart. I, with my ability, cannot find the right verb to describe my feeling. It is like the peacefulness when a baby in its mother's bosom meets the mother's eyes while listening to her heartbeat. Even this description cannot fully capture my experience. Then, as God's calling voice changes, the brightness of the beautiful light changes, and I go into an ecstatic state. My whole body seems to be melting. Then, suddenly, I am standing by myself: I cannot see God.

How does such an enrapturing light come to visit a human being instantaneously and continually? God's love manifested as light feels different from moment to moment. Brilliant lights, large or small, and round-shaped as if in a fireworks display, come to human beings as lights of love, varying in splendor. The sentiment we can feel from the light differs according to the shape of radiating light. In addition to the love I have experienced, I have seen God's love shown to other persons. And yet, God is the essence of love.

## The Image of God Is Fire and Light

Based upon what can we tell, that light is the shape of love. Because the image of God is fire and light, the elements of love in the human mind interact immediately when God's light is received. Just as light is turned on when you press a switch, when you see God's light, love can start operating and turn your heart into love itself.

## The Reason for the Gateway of the Blessing to be Opened Wide.

God's original Will for human beings was for them to maintain the qualities with which they were originally created. But due to the fall, the original parents' descendants could not be born with natural love. God was heartbroken to see His children born with a heart moving in two different directions, being wrongly structured. Therefore, in order to solve the problems of having a heart with two directions and of having further departed from the original plan of restoration and God's authority, as described in the history of restoration, we have to go through the course of rebirth. By being born again without original sin (we can take after the essence of love God as originally desired), then we can experience the complete love of God. This is why we have to be reborn through True Parents. That is the Blessing. This explains why, recently, the True Parents widened the gateway for the Blessing, granting such incredible benefit.

Though recipients do not understand it, once they receive the great favor by participating in the Blessing, they become blessed people. In addition to that, while the True Parents are on earth, endlessly opening the way for myriad people to receive this special favor, those who receive the favor are the Heavenly people. Since they go through the course of rebirth, this is the period when the descendants of the people on earth can receive fortune and blessings without their having establishing any conditions.

## Love Is God's Biggest Gift

Love is the core of God's image received by human beings when they are born. Human beings should inherit God's love as is. However, having gone wrong, the relationship with God was disconnected. To re-establish this relationship, human beings should resemble God. The best way to resemble God is to restore the original image of love as sons and daughters. Love! Love! Love! It is the fundamental power with which we can overcome and melt down every difficulty, and thus accomplish everything. Love is the biggest gift we received from God and the sealed proof that we are His children. Love! We have to strive and exert ourselves to find the love we lost.

# CHAPTER THREE

# LIFE IN THE SPIRIT WORLD
# VIEWED FROM THE PRINCIPLE

## SUBJECT AND OBJECT
## (LAW OF THE SPIRIT WORLD)      JULY 21, 1997

*Subject*

When a subject and object desire the give and take of love and beauty, the universal prime force endowed by God and ruled by God operates and becomes the fundamental force for their reciprocation. The subject uses it to give force to the object, and the object uses it to return force to the subject. Thus it exists within the forces of action that form a reciprocal relationship between a subject and an object. It does not work independently, but is given by God, by whom we sustain our life and continue to exist. There is nothing that can exist independently. Existence itself can be possible only through the force generated from give and take actions between a subject and an object. Therefore, whether in the spirit world or on earth, the forces of all existing beings are manifested through the process of reciprocal relationship between a subject and an object.

At this point, I would like to write down the actions of a subject and an object that I witnessed in the spirit world. In the spirit world, when God, who is in the position of subject, gives to a spirit person, in the position of an object, His force is immediately reflected in the spirit person and they are united. For example, when God calls my name, "Sang Hun!" in a nonverbal way, I, His object, with an original mind, am automatically drawn to His order. I would not question Him or express my own views, such as, "God, what is it?" "I do not know," "I do

49

not understand," etc., but I am automatically drawn to Him. This can be compared to a northern magnetic force being drawn to a southern magnetic force.

Therefore, when we come before God, human beings are attracted to Him as if they were His shadow, in the relationship of subject and object. This is the fundamental force in accordance with the original principle of reciprocation. Which is stronger between the force that a subject gives to an object and the force that an object returns to a subject is not a question. The important question is how they can have give and take at the same level of force. Since God gives human beings the universal prime force, we are to live according to the original Will God had at the time of His creating.

Therefore, the fundamental force of the universal prime force can bring smooth give and take actions only when a subject and an object establish a standard as a reciprocal base. If a subject and an object, whether in the human, animal, plant or mineral realm, form a standard for reciprocation, the force of multiplication comes into being. If there is instead conflict or friction, an action of force does not take place. Therefore, since God is the original standard for the fundamental force that is required for us to exist, if we have an attitude through which we live attending God in our mind, we can immediately receive the force of the subject and reflect the same force as an object.

## Object

The force of an object should be like a beam generator, immediately returning force at the same time as receiving the fundamental force. This means that when a subject appears as the fundamental force that is received from God, its object can also receive the same force. Therefore, a subject and an object should neither be in the position of relating to each other independently, nor follow the rule that one must give first and the other next in an orderly manner. They should have a reciprocal relationship on the same level. In a reciprocal standard there is no concern for priority of position or level. A conflict that arises from a disunited husband and a wife, who cannot become one as subject and object, is not a fundamental force given by God. It is from fallen nature.

Subject and object have been derailed from the right track, losing the original force from God and deviating from the realm of God's dominion. Accordingly, since an object is reflected by the action of its subject's fundamental force, it should not deviate from the direction of the original force that strives to respond to its subject from the position of an object. If an object has deviated from receiving force from its subject, the object should strive to have its own force establish a reciprocal circuit.

Let me give you an example. In terms of the relationship between a husband and a wife, a husband is in the position of a subject. Yet if something goes wrong with the husband, the wife comes to stand in the position of the subject, the original positions being reversed, until the husband returns to his original position, which takes time.

## The Main Topic

When a subject and an object have a good reciprocal relationship, the force of original value can be manifested. However, if something goes wrong with one party, and thus their position is reversed, until the one party returns to the original state, the other party should keep his or her position.

Otherwise, the fundamental force given by God will leave them and be lost. Therefore, in order for a subject and an object to have proper give and take actions, they should serve and attend God, the original source of the force.

Since all beings sustain their lives by the force generated between a subject and an object, unless two become one, both of them will walk a path of destruction and death. Both subject and object must strive to unite, always examining themselves as to whether they love the original force or are accustomed to the fallen nature. If they are crossing a bridge made of stone, they should take with care each step toward the world of eternity. Then they will be able to lead a life of wisdom.

## There Are No Exceptions to Spiritual Laws

Many people understand that the fundamental force from God is the universal prime force. Yet people do not think about how they can possess the force themselves. During their earthly life, they should realize the value of the original force. The rays of the original force can be reflected only when one is on the original rail, not off the rail. Even when you are on the rail, you should take care not to be derailed. In the spirit world, no exceptions and no forgiveness are applied. On earth, we can be forgiven based on circumstances or heartistic relations, but in the spirit world, even in the case of a parent-child relationship, that is not acceptable. This is not because the spiritual laws are fussy, but because everything is done in accordance with the Principle.

You might wonder if the God of love should not be more understanding. However, because He is the subject of the original love, if He allows exceptions, the fundamental order will be destroyed. In other words, He must refuse them in order to maintain a right order in the world of eternity. Thus, it is because He loves us that He does not forgive us. Therefore, we should live each moment fully for the life of eternity. The reason why I am saying this is to fulfill my obligation of helping the True Parents as their son when they reorganize the spirit world. If we are truly their children, should we not live a life of filial piety, helping our parents when they are in difficulties?

*Since what is seen in the spirit world is so clear, Dr. Sang Hun Lee seems to be emphasizing his views, after analyzing his observations and experiences. (Medium: Y.S. Kim)*

## THREE OBJECTS PURPOSE          *JULY 28, 1997*

*Three Objects Purpose*

The three objects purpose is God's precious blessing and gift to human beings, given them at the time He created them. This principle came into being to make possible a condition for human beings to come before God. However, due to the Fall, the principle of the love and beauty that should have been reciprocated between us as husband and wife was invaded. In order to restore us to the original state centered on God, we should reverse the wrong fulfillment of the three objects purpose, dating from the time of Adam and Eve. Centered on God, Adam and Eve should have had a reciprocal relationship of love and beauty. However, because their relationship was centered on Satan, the circuit of the original reciprocal relationship was destroyed. Therefore, God intends to build the ideal of the kingdom of heaven based on love, by restoring human beings so as to attain the value of the original standard of the three objects purpose.

## The Completion of a Couple

One of God's blessings to us human beings is the multiplication of children. This is Agape-type love that gives and gives without any conditions attached. That type of love is not often experienced in our life. However, like a spring of water that never dries up, the love of God, who desires to give infinitely as the King of love, never dries up. As a husband and a wife, we should resemble God's love and become one with His love that constantly desires to give and give. Then our love and beauty will be returned to God as a precious offering. How many couples exist on earth today actually practicing and living God's love according to His desire?

The kingdom of heaven in spirit world is a beautiful place where a couple lives, returning love and beauty to God and reaching the standard of the three objects purpose. Therefore, there can be no deceptions or falsities in the couple's loving. Since the conjugal love is given and returned centered on God, it should have the standard of supreme value. During the earthly life, a couple should live a life that is totally united with God's true love that fulfills the three objects purpose. Otherwise, even if we go to spirit world, we cannot possess the love of the kingdom of heaven.

## FALLEN NATURE                    JULY 28, 1997

### Fallen Nature Is...

Fallen nature refers to a mentality that is derailed from the original track of the Principle that God originally intended. Then, how can human beings return to the original track of the

Principle, removing the fallen nature? The reason why God loves us without any reasons or conditions is simply because we are His children. Human beings who are derailed from the original track should return to the original position as God's children. However, to do this is impossible without establishing a proper condition.

Then, what is that condition? When human beings created as the children of God fell, by being derailed from the original track, they came to serve another master, resulting in their attending two masters. However, they should clearly realize that God is the true master. That is, only when they return to God after leaving their position of dealing with two masters, can they be fully restored.

## Rebirth

Complete restoration is simple. Within human beings, who deviated from the original track of the Principle, leaving their original position as children of God, fallen blood is flowing. Therefore, fallen activities should be stopped. However, in order to be reborn, we should understand the process of rebirth. Our defiled lineage should be completely sanctified, through a process called rebirth, and we should inherit the love of God. In order to be reborn, our body needs to re-enter the womb. This may sound like a fantasy; however, the Principle teaches us that we can go back to God through establishing an indemnity condition of lesser value.

Then, we need a mediator, which is the True Parents. Human beings cannot go to God without the True Parents since the original sin can be removed only through the True Parents. Only through them can fallen human beings come forward to God as His original children, with God-like value. Since we inherited the original sin with fallen nature from Satan, we should be separated from it. It is wrong to think that we can do this on our own. Separation from the original sin is possible when we realize the value of the Blessing given by True Parents. From this perspective, we can learn that the Blessing contains many meanings. After coming to spirit world, I realized even more deeply the amazing value and greatness of our True Parents.

## THE FOUR-POSITION FOUNDATION                    JULY 31, 1997

*What Is the Four-Position Foundation?*

The four-position foundation means a foundation where a subject and an object have united and multiplied centering on God. Human beings who are created as children of God based upon His purpose of creation, and who are supposed to follow His ideal of "subject and object," should grow up within the sphere of God's love and fulfill the ideal of creation God originally intended. However, Satan became the dominator of this world. So, the ideal world can be built when the world under Satan's dominion is restored and completely brought under the dominion of God. God, through His providence of restoration, has been looking for the human beings to build heaven on Earth. When the people on Earth come back to God's bosom, the eternal kingdom of heaven in the spirit world, centering on God, will be built.

*True Parents of Heaven and Earth.*

God wanted to build the ideal world. However, the world became evil due to the human Fall. Further, the course of the history of restoration became entangled. The providence for restoration is to untie the knots of resentments and sorrows of history one by one, and through doing this bring the world under the dominion of God. A master who can bring to its end this providence for restoration should come to this world. Then the establishment of heaven can begin. The one is the True Parent. The history of salvation for humankind initiated by the True Parents has greatly contributed to the development of human history. Through this fundamental providence, an eternal ideal world can be established here in the spirit world.

Since the True Parents who are now on earth are True Parents not only for the physical world but also for the spirit world, they are the masters of the eternal Sabbath of the spirit world and they are the masters of the ideal kingdom of heaven. Therefore, spirit persons in some levels have lived with the hope of the day when the True Parents come to the spirit world and build the ideal world here. The spirit persons in high levels know of the coming world of hope, but spirit persons in low levels don't know how their present, terrifying world of punishment will change. For them, there is no hope and nothing to wait for. There is only continual pain and suffering.

Therefore, the greater the number of people going to hell, the more the spirit world will be complicated and the more True Parents will have to work after they come to spirit world. Even though the external Blessing seems to be given freely, the destiny of those who were headed toward hell will change. So, let's become pioneers who will build the eternal world. That is the way to fulfill our filial piety. In conclusion, completion of the four-position foundation is the completion of the kingdom of heaven. The completion of the ideal kingdom of heaven is to show our filial devotion to True Parents.

## THE IDEAL OF HEAVEN                    *AUGUST 7, 1997*

*Heaven*

Heaven is the place where people who have received recognition as God's children gather. They are the owners of heaven. The ideal heaven is realized by those who live for the sake of others and do not think or act for themselves.

What is the proper behavior in heaven? In heaven, people's behavior is motivated by their own humble attitude, not by someone else.

Is there a fence in heaven? It is not a place where someone asks you to come or go. It is not the place where someone makes an order. Rather, it is the place where people act by knowing and feeling God's breath.

There are no classes in heaven—no such rule that someone is higher or lower than others are. This place doesn't care about people's social position. The one who was at the highest position and the one who was at the lowest position are united by their love for each other. In heaven, there is no such a gruesome scene where the lower kisses up to the higher as on earth. The one who accomplishes the ideal of the kingdom of heaven is the one who knows God's ideal and realizes God's fundamental will and lives it. The laws of the spirit world are very strict. Examination is very exacting. So people on earth should try to live looking forward to living in the ideal kingdom of heaven.

*The Principle of Reciprocity and the Ideal*
*of the Kingdom of Heaven*

The principle of reciprocity can be explained through the principle of give and take action. The meaning of give and take action is not only to give and take well. The parties also should know upon whom the action is centered. A subject and an object shouldn't pursue their own ideals centering on themselves. They should realize that the sure guide toward God and the ideal of heaven is to live in one direction through the circuit of their give and take action. That direction is toward the owner of the fundamental power. The subjective force in the principle of reciprocity is generated when it is for the sake of its object, and the objective power is generated when it is for the sake of its subject. These forces are the fundamental forces following the principle of reciprocity, which directs the forces to be directed to God. I'd like to say that the realization of heaven is the main purpose of the "principle of reciprocity."

## Gateways to Heaven

There are many gateways through which one must pass before entering the kingdom of heaven. Heaven is the storage where you collect all the fruits of your life. Here, they measure the weight of your bundle and see how much recognition you can get. In other words, they compare the weight of the good and of the evil you have done. What was your earthly life? Was it for God? Was it for you? What were your views of the world and your country? What did you leave behind on earth?

These things are taken into consideration. There are so many such examinations and they examine your life in full detail. It is like water collected from a river finally coming to your dinner table after being sterilized and filtered so many times. It is not that a guard questions you and takes you to a certain gate. My experience is that I go to this gateway and that gateway as if attracted by a magnet, and I must pass through each of them. The pain when you reach a certain gateway and are rejected because of your sin is beyond description.

It is so shameful and fearful.

There are so many levels behind each gateway. There are many more places than simply heaven, Paradise and hell to which we refer on earth. Then, how can we safely pass through all gateways and go to heaven? If there are some gateways you cannot pass due to your sins, you will spend a certain time there to pay indemnity, with the length of time based upon the condition of God's special Blessing, the achievements of your descendants, prayer, offering, service, and so on. Spirit persons are waiting for the True Parents to come to the spirit world, when they will build new standards for passing through each gateway. I am really worried that this will be more work for the True Parents.

# FORMATION OF THE FOUR-POSITION FOUNDATION AND DUAL CHARACTERISTICS

*Formation*

The four-position foundation is the core of the Divine Principle, which teaches that a couple should be united centering on their love and multiply children. However, the formation of the four-position foundation when viewed in the spirit world is much more exciting and mysterious. The four-position foundation does mean that a husband and a wife are united and multiply their children centering on God; however, when they are in love and united with each other, there is no distinction of subject and object. They completely become one body. More than that, God's love covers their love, so that the only thing visible to us is resplendent light. The beauty of love itself is the only thing that can be seen.

## The Ideal of Unity in Love

Then how does children's love look? Children's love results in unity just as a couple's love does. Parents and children are united into one with their love. Even though they are three distinct people—father, mother and child—they do not appear separately when they are united in love. Their union could appear as the father's figure, the mother's figure, or the children's figure. However, once they start to talk to each other, they appear again as different people. The formation of the four-position foundation means that if we are united centering on God, we will be one body with God. Therefore, there don't appear here four separate existences (including God), although they seem that way on earth.

A couple united with God lives as one body even though they are two different people. This is how the spirit persons at the highest level appear. However, a subject and an object that are not fully united do not appear as one. Neither can God's resplendent light be seen in them. Only people who pass all the gateways to heaven can achieve such unity. Therefore, the basis of the four-position foundation is that a couple manifesting dual characteristics is united in their love for God. The four-position foundation is God's fundamental purpose, and it is the foundation for God's fundamental power of love to exist and operate in the world.

# UNIVERSAL PRIME ENERGY, GIVE AND TAKE ACTION, AND THE PRINCIPLE OF RECIPROCITY VIEWED IN TERMS OF THE PRINCIPLE OF DUAL CHARACTERISTICS    AUGUST 4, 1997

Dual characteristics means that figures in the created world resemble God's characteristics. God gives their characteristics. The fundamental force of it is "Universal Prime Energy," and "give and take action" is the action between these two characteristics. Then, what is the Principle of Reciprocity? When a subject and an object carry on "give and take action," the force of "give and take action" (Universal Prime Energy) causes them to have give and take with each other. In other words, this force is like the attraction of a magnet.

Divine Principle describes this, the utmost fundamental energy, as "a subject consisting of the dual characteristics," or universal prime energy or give and take action. However, the origin is the same. It can be simply said and understood as "God's fundamental energy." The fundamental force for the changing of the seasons is not formed by human beings. The originating force of all energy used in the created world stems from only one force, given by God. We cannot truly explicate the energy for the existence of the eternal God. That is the energy of God, my Father, who is the sole creator of humankind.

God is the master of the spirit world, which is limitlessly wide, which our reason cannot understand, which we cannot see with our physical senses, and which we cannot grasp or explain. You cannot describe God, no matter how long you study Him. He is the One who cannot be described nor explained in terms of any of our senses or emotions. I, Sang Hun Lee, like logical reason and analysis, but God is the master of the eternal light that cannot be divided nor analyzed. God is the One who guides the providence and leads people profoundly with His resplendent light.

*Oh! My God*

I thought I could analyze God if I came to spirit world. However, since coming to the spirit world, I am just full of admiration for its huge scale, and my expectation that I could analyze the spirit world seems stupid. "My God, please forgive this son. You are the One who cannot be compared with anything else, anywhere. Your value and existence is one and only, incomparable, Heavenly Father. There is no other way to express my feeling other than "Oh! My God! Oh! My God! Oh! My God! Please forgive me." Therefore, one who tries to analyze and study God is the most stupid person. The wisest man only says "My Heavenly Father," and realizes that the fundamental source of all energy is the expression of the Heavenly Father's prime energy, as explained in the Divine Principle.

## HUMAN STRUCTURE BASED ON SUBJECT AND OBJECT RELATIONSHIP                    *AUGUST 4, 1997*

*Human Structure*

According to the structure of a human being, a person isn't created to live individually. He or she is supposed to live for the existence of his or her subject or object. When a subject and object perform give and take action well and become one, they form a foundation through which God can work and they become the ultimate object of joy of God. Most people's lives are full of thinking simply to live for their own sake. However, living individually does not agree with the original Will of God. For that reason, a person pursuing a single life is not a filial child of God, but is one of the people who become ashamed when in the spirit world. If human beings were structured to live singly, God's creation, though reflecting the highest intelligence, would be called a failure.

### Life for the Spouse

Since a human being is God's ultimate creation, the human being must possess the element God most desires. This is the heart with which a person cannot help caring for a spouse. Therefore, according to the external dual structure of humankind, a person needs a complement, and the person's internal character is formed with the heart of caring for the complement. A human being is supposed to live according to the direction to live for others given by God. If a man or woman goes against this direction, it will be a crime in front of God, and he or she will have no home in the spirit world. Since no one can live on earth forever, he or she will become lost. For that reason, a person should appreciate the value of life given by God and live a life to serve God and others.

## MEDIUM OF LOVE                    AUGUST 4, 1997

### Man Is the Center of Love

Since a man has dual structure, he should be the center of love to be completed in front of God. In other words, God created man with the highest intelligence, distinct from the other creations, and for that reason, man should be an existence more valuable than other creations. Because of the Fall, man could not accomplish that. Therefore, he must fulfill his responsibility as a true child by following the direction to return to the original position. Why is this? God makes the creation. Its value is merely to offer its beauty and growth to God.

### Man Is the Medium of Love

God has provided man with the value of love, which other creations do not possess. Love cannot be generated by a single existence. Its value can emerge only when a subject and object are united and become one. A human being, which is a medium of love, becomes the center of love and leads God to the ultimate joy by being qualified as a true child. Thus, man should be the medium of love to offer the ultimate love to God and lead God to His joy. Man should reach the standard of value that God provided. Man should do his best to live his life in order to make God joyful. To do that, we each should love our spouse. We should become one and be God's children returning glory to Him. That is the perfection of man.

## TRUE LOVE                    *AUGUST 7, 1997*

### True Love

True love is the original love which was lost in the Garden of Eden and which we try to find in order to live with God. Love can be called true love only when its standard of value is centered on God. There is no true love without God. Because Adam and Eve didn't offer the first fruit of love to God, God and human beings have lived as parents and children of sadness. Because Satan took the first fruit of love, God has worked in order to take it back. However, since countless sinful seeds have already been planted on the earth, God is working to collect the pure grain after harvesting the fruit of sin, by sifting the grain.

God needs a strategy for bringing back the first fruit that was taken away by Satan. It involves the condition for indemnity. Since the True Parents came to the earth, God's formula has been bringing its final results. This is because the ultimate purpose of God's restoration providence is to regain His lost children. Humankind must realize original true love and return true love to God. Only those who have been selected to attain the True Parents' standard of rebirth through the Blessing can appear as true children of God.

Those who have not passed the procedure of the Blessing are not qualified as first fruits. In order to be guided to God by original true love, the couple who received the Blessing from the True Parents must love each other, multiply children and establish the four-position foundation. True Love results in the couple becoming one, and the parents and children becoming one through loving each other centering on God.

## The Appearance of True Love Is a Luminary of the Light

In the spirit world, true love appears as radiating perfected light. The lustrous light can be radiated from children or from parents. The original luminary of the light is the true incarnation of true love that God has given us. If a husband and a wife cannot become one, and children cannot become one, the light of true love cannot be radiated completely. We have usually conceived of true love as agape love that we give and receive eternally. However, the fullness of true love is given through the four-position foundation of complete oneness centering on God. Therefore, those who have not been reborn cannot join the line of complete true love. Thus, they do not have a ticket to come to the kingdom of heaven in the spirit world. Everyone should do his or her best to participate in the line of the Blessing.

## ORIGINAL LOVE                              AUGUST 7, 1997

*Original Love*

God said it is beautiful watching Adam and Eve loving each other. God rejoiced even to the degree of feeling rapture. However, because of the Fall of humankind, God had lost all such love. For this reason, humankind has the responsibility of consoling God's grieving heart and of letting Him again rejoice. I mentioned original love when discussing true love. Now I will categorize the appearances of original love. These are a) the love of a husband and a wife centering on God; b) the love of children centering on God; and c) true love centered on God.

*Appearance of an Original Couple*
*Standing in Front of God*

What is the appearance of a couple who have established the original love when both finally come to kingdom of heaven and are meeting God? They come to the spirit world just as a bridegroom and bride enter the wedding hall, wearing the most beautiful clothing on earth. As the bridegroom and bride whom God receives are extremely beautiful, the scene brings to my mind the image of an angel from heaven having descended to the earth. The good man and good woman go forward to God and offer a full bow while receiving resplendent light within a beautiful melody. Within the bright radiance of light, the husband and wife embrace each other. The appearance of the couple loving is as the world of light becoming one, and is very bright. Within the light, God embraces them and rejoices by radiating love in a stem of light.

The bride who came to the spirit world before her bridegroom goes forward to God when she finally receives her bridegroom. This is a description of the time when Sang Hun Lee was going forward to God. This made me think that this was the original love of God which God wanted to establish in the Garden of Eden.

## PRINCIPLE OF RECIPROCITY IN THE VIEW OF ORIGINAL LOVE *AUGUST 8, 1997*

*Foundation of the Principle of Reciprocity*

Original love is the love that God wanted to develop in the Garden of Eden. Then, how does it relate to the Principle of Relationship? The foundation of the Principle of Relationship is giving and receiving for the sake of the other. What I want to say about the Principle of Relationship in view of original love concerns the kingdom of heaven made up of good men and good women in the spirit world.

*Life of an Original Couple in the View of the Principle of Relationship*

What is the life like here of an original couple in view of the Principle of Relationship? As an example, let's say there is a couple eating together at a meal table. If there is a specific food that the wife wants to offer her husband, at the instant of her thought, the food is put in front of her husband. When her husband feels gratitude toward his wife, at that instant she recognizes his feeling and smiles.

However, I have seen that people eating in hell do not recognize each other's thoughts. Rather, hell is as in a prison where people are fighting each other for food because of their hunger. In the kingdom of heaven, couples know each other's thoughts, words and actions by simply looking into each other's eyes. Since they always know each other's heart of wanting to give and the heart of willingness to give, they correspond just as a magnet and compass correspond. Accordingly, they are always very humble to each other; they always express respect to each other; and they live always showing warm and peaceful smiles.

The world of original love is the world where couples live with the heart of willingness to give and receive centering on God, and dance within the rapturous light of God as one does in the warm sunlight of spring. Couples on earth are dreaming of the ideal of original love. I want you to live a life that can be accepted by God.

## DOMINION OVER THE UNIVERSE
## AND THE VALUE OF MANKIND  *AUGUST 8, 1998*

*Humankind Is the Primary Agent*
*over the Entire World of Creation*

God, who created heaven and earth, created humankind as the primary agent over the entire world of creation. However, because of the Fall of humankind, it seems that the value of all things and the value of humankind was reversed. For this reason, humankind lost the value of existence as the children of God. How painful God feels that the world of creation He built for the sake of His children grows and multiplies on its own, but the primary agent of the creation of heaven and earth is not appearing. Man's task is to correct his fallen position and return to God by getting onto the original track.

However, the only way for humankind to appear as the owner in front of all things is by standing on the standard of the value of the Blessing, by being reborn through True Parents. God originally blessed man to do whatever he desired in the Garden of Eden. That is, God allowed him the qualification of manager of the entire world of creation. Through rebirth, man can regain his role as the primary agent in the Garden, and attain the standard of value of the manager of the universe. Then, how high does the standard of value of humankind reach? It is as the children of God and the owner of the entire world of creation. God created all things for the sake of humankind. Therefore, God rejoices only when humankind rejoices together with God as they survey all things.

## The Appearance of Man and All Things in Harmony

Don't you think that a reciprocal relationship must be established between man and physical things, since they are his objects of joy? Then, let's give an example of how the harmony of all things and human beings, who are the primary agents of the universe, appears in the spirit world. When a couple embraces, grass, flowers and birds surrounding them each harmonize with them. A blade of grass radiates beautiful colors. It swings light with excitement. Birds gather and sing their own beautiful songs. A passing breeze harmonizes with the couple by bestowing a silky soft touch. Everything around them radiates in beauty. When the couple makes love within such an atmosphere, God answers with a stream of bright rays of light. You might imagine a scene in a movie in which the king and queen in a castle, wearing soft and beautiful clothes, make love while beautiful harp music is heard. However, that cannot compare with true love in heaven. Man received an abundance of treasures from God as the manager of all things. However, because of the Fall, he cannot feel or see them. Yet, if we attain the standard of the value of a perfected human, we will restore every relationship. Therefore, man must again realize his value as the original owner of the entire universe and return gratitude and glory to God.

## DOMINION OVER THE UNIVERSE AND GOD'S TRUE LOVE    *AUGUST 8, 1997*

### We Are God's Children

God created humankind as His children. God cannot but have a painful heart toward His children when they do not return to God's bosom and instead wander around at a distance. For this reason, there are times when God reverses the management indirectly. By doing so, God has been consoled through patiently watching all things. However, God feels joy when His children appear in front of all things as the primary agent. This is because all things desire human beings to have dominion over them.

### God's Joy and Love

When God sees the environment harmonize while the couple appears in front of Him and returns joy and glory to Him, He wants to bless them by saying that the world of creation is all theirs. One stream of brilliant light harmonizes with all things and reconfirms that the primary agent in such a beautiful world is humankind. Then God blesses the couple to harvest as they want. When a good man and good woman having received that Blessing walk by, each blade of grass dances with joy. The couple feels God's love within the beautiful, enraptured atmosphere wherein birds rejoice with their own chirping sounds, melody wafts on the breeze, and indescribable fragrance fills the air. Therefore, since the world of creation is the expression of God's devoted love that is given to us, we must joyfully return our love to God as primary agents over the world of creation.

## PERFECTED HUMAN BEINGS
## HAVE THE VALUE OF GOD          *AUGUST 8, 1997*

*Perfected Man Is God's Heir*

When man grows in the right way, being completely accepted by God as His child, he becomes a perfected child of God and is bequeathed everything. Thus, man, who is recognized as the manager of the world of creation, can stand as the object of God's eternal joy. Such a person has the standard of heart that can know God's thought through living and rejoicing with God. He has attained the standard of the value of God.

*One Who Lives with God*

For this reason, indeed, man is to attain the position of having the value of God, and this is God's ultimate desire for man. God wants man to be in the perfected position, where God can bless him with the words, "These are all yours. You have done everything." That is the position where we always live with God within God's radiance.

# CAIN AND ABEL
# IN VIEW OF THE
# PRINCIPLE OF RECIPROCITY    AUGUST 9, 1997

## The Relationship Between Cain and Abel

Already, the origin of the Principle of Reciprocation was mentioned several times. Here, I will discuss how the relationship between Cain and Abel is systemized in the spirit world in view of the Principle of Reciprocation. God was going to give Cain the exact same love He gave Abel, if and when Cain and Abel established a standard for reciprocation through Cain respecting and loving Abel. However, rather than loving Abel, Cain was arrogant, showing off his qualification as the elder son. This pained Abel's heart, and stimulated his anger toward Cain. Cain's arrogant behavior resulted in a sorrowful history within God's providence.

God has had to re-indemnify segments of history due to mistakes. God has pulled man by letting man establish the condition for receiving the Messiah and then stand in the position where God can say that he has no sin. Then according to the Principle of Reciprocation, by which the subject and object become one with the love caused by the heart of wanting to give to each other, the restored original relationship of Cain and Abel will be the same as if man had not fallen. Cain will not have the emotion of hating Abel to the extent of wanting to kill him. On the contrary, the power of respecting and helping each other will function more strongly.

## The Cain and Abel Relationship in Heaven

The Cain and Abel relationship clearly exists in spirit world. There are Cain-Abel relationships, such as elder person, younger person, higher-level person, lower-level person, one who receives more love closer to God, one who receives less love of God, etc. For example, between the elder person and younger person, rather than the elder person ignoring the other's feelings and giving orders by screaming, he will ask, "What are you doing now?" with a warm heart. Then the younger person will smile and respond, "How shall I help you?" In such an atmosphere, their hearts have give and take. Also, when a younger person has a question for the elder person, he will ask, "I am very curious about such and such content. Could you help me understand?" Then the elder person answers not with an attitude of authority and reputation, but with the love of a true elder brother.

God did not apply the Principle of Reciprocation between subject and object to humankind alone. To every creature, God gave the heart of love that wants to give for the sake of the other. Since such a heartistic relationship has been broken, the Cain and Abel relationship became one of distance. Because the situation on earth became complicated, the situation in spirit world became more complicated. The ideal of the kingdom of heaven must first be realized on earth, and on that foundation the spirit world will become perfectly organized. I want you to live your life on earth through reorganizing, rethinking and reestablishing the original Principle of Reciprocation.

## THE KINGDOM OF HEAVEN  *AUGUST 9, 1997*

*What Is the Kingdom of Heaven?*

In simple words, the kingdom of heaven is the place where the people who have no individualism or self-centered thought gather and live. In other words, it can be summarized as the world of living together and glorifying together, with the heart of willingness to live for the sake of the other, willingness to give endlessly.

*What Is Hell?*

Hell is the place where people are gathered who have an attachment to "I," the individual, to my situation, and to my possessions. Hell is the world where persons with such thought go.

*The World of Eternity*

Generally, most people living on earth pursue physical pleasure as their ideal of life. This is the reason that life in the physical world, not knowing God, can easily become preparation for hell. The world of eternity is unavoidable for everyone. For this reason, considering the eternal world, we must live our short physical lives with daily examination. The law of the eternal world accepts no excuses. There are no personal explanations. This is the content that Sang Hun Lee truly wants to communicate, so as to help the people on earth, and this may be my best gift. All I want to mention again and again is, "for the sake of eternity, do not live in the moment foolishly." That is the way of filial piety to the True Parents.

## LIFE IN THE KINGDOM
## OF HEAVEN                              *AUGUST 9, 1997*

The kingdom of heaven is the area in which we become one with each other's love centering on God. In this world, each person respects the other's personality, is always humble, always warm, and always smiles. Your height, your beauty, your position, your wealth, your education do not matter at all. In this world, there is no difficulty and no envy, but only eternal happiness.

# CHAPTER FOUR

# MEETINGS IN THE SPIRIT WORLD I

## JESUS CHRIST                    AUGUST 10, 1997

You are all concerned about Jesus staying in Paradise. Then, what does Jesus do? He lives as if he were the only existing person in the cosmos. What does that mean? It means that he feels extremely lonely. There are many Christians around Jesus. Some are wearing crosses; some are holding rosaries. However, even though Christians serve Jesus, fulfilling the highest goal of their earthly lives, Jesus feels lonely. What is the reason for this? If, as Christians believe, Jesus is the Christ of glory, why is he staying in Paradise? It is because Jesus is still praying and working for the complete fulfillment of God's will on earth. Since most Christians do not really understand his heart, he is in a lonely position with which we should sympathize. From this perspective, even Paradise is not a perfectly happy place. So, Christians who are in Paradise beg Jesus to take them forward to the door of the kingdom of heaven. "Oh! Our Lord! We want to go together with you!" They are begging like that. Whenever they do so, Jesus feels pain in his heart. He answers, "I stay here because I am God's son, but my mission as Christ is continuing, and I am happy to be in this place."

Then, when will Christians be able to move from Paradise to the kingdom of heaven? Until when will Jesus stay there? He will wait until the True Parents come for liberation. At that time, the people in Paradise will be able to receive many advantages.

I often saw Jesus walking together with God, but many

Christians did not recognize that Jesus was with God. This is one difference between Paradise and the kingdom of heaven, where everyone will understand Jesus and God.

## THE HOLY MOTHER MARY     AUGUST 10, 1997

The Holy Mother Mary was a great woman who is respected as Jesus' mother. Even though she is always with Jesus in Paradise, she displays humility and a sense of unworthiness in front of him. She lives with a burdened conscience because she did not fulfill her entire responsibility for Jesus on Earth. Even though she was not a nun, she now lives as a nun. Therefore, the relationship between Jesus and his mother is not easy. Nonetheless, there is no blame between them, and they relate with great care for each other.

## JOSEPH     AUGUST 10, 1997

Joseph, Holy Mother Mary's husband, lives in the same level as Mary, but he is also living a very lonely life in separation from Mary. Even though they were a couple on Earth, now they live as strangers and do not even meet. Joseph feels it would cause difficulty if he met Jesus, and even the Holy Mother Mary also feels apologetic meeting Jesus. Moreover, they seem to worry about what people think of them. Joseph is repenting for his past earthly life and feels very sorry to Jesus. Because most people who are around them know of the relationship between Joseph and Mary, they feel pressure and tension. We can see that Paradise is not a superficially happy or dazzling place; rather, it is the place of hope and desire.

# BUDDHA                    *AUGUST 11, 1997*

Buddha is the most famous and respected personage for Buddhists. I am going to tell the story of meeting Buddha. He was spending his time sitting at the foot of a high mountain and sighing deeply. When I asked him why he sighs so much and has so many concerns, he answered, "You did not come here to meet me, but came to analyze me. Since you are living in God's love, you may know every situation. In spite of that, why do you ask me? On every April 8, Buddhists celebrate my birthday with a festival, but I have only the heart to want to hide. I feel very sorry and repent that when I lived on earth, I did not teach how to serve God. Because I also refused to acknowledge God, my teaching seems to lead many people astray. What can I do?"

He spoke to me like this, with deep sighing. His face does not seem to look bright and he likes to walk in the high mountains. He dislikes meeting people and wants to go where nobody is. He is always repenting in his prayer and continues to offer full bows before God with a completely sincere mind. Even though some Buddhist believers are following him, he does not appear in places where many people are gathered. Finally, the place where Buddha is living seems to be the highest level of the middle spirit world. I am going to share the Divine Principle and Unification Thought lectures with Buddha continuously.

His character is very mild and humble. He does not walk proudly with an uplifted head, but drops his head at a 45-degree angle. He always talks with a benevolent face. When he was listening to a lecture, he continuously thanked me for my lecture. When I ask him to make a promise for the next lecture, he does not promise easily. After a few silent moments, he makes a facial expression as if to say, "If you have extra time, please come." He does not say any unnecessary words. He is very humble and benevolent.

How can Buddha meet God? Some Buddhists may believe that he was the highest religious founder on earth and so he should be treated most highly. However, even though it may be a very troubling story for Buddhists, he cannot meet God directly. However, he can sometimes receive God's direction through a messenger. When he is to receive God's direction, then as a servant does before a king, he gives a full bow before God and kneels down to receive it. Then he gives another full bow as he receives God's direction, as one does in reading a king's order. Buddhists can sometimes witness such a scene, but they do not know what is taking place. Moreover, God's direction does not come often.

The contents of God's direction seem to be comforting to Buddha, as he knows he will need to wait silently for a long time until he can come into the direct realm of God's love. It was very surprising that God is walking with Jesus but not with Buddha directly. Why is that so? Jesus is the Son of God, but because Buddha is not, he is in the realm of the Fall, without the fundamental condition to go before God. However, God forgives him and consoles him.

## CONFUCIUS                                   AUGUST 11, 1997

Confucius is the great King of Confucianism. He stays in the same level as Buddha, which is the highest level of the middle spirit world. Even in the coldest winter, he wears the classical oriental overcoat and hat, and has deep meditation, sitting on the snow for several hours. Therefore, if I do not make an appointment with him, it is not easy to meet him.

When I greeted him saying, "I came here to meet teacher Confucius," he responded, "Isn't it rude if you come here without an appointment?" I introduced myself to him. "When I was living on earth, I thought of your Confucianism as a most valuable thought, and I wrote Unification Thought, and I lived having a new view of life through the Reverend Moon's teaching."

When I had finished introducing myself, he said, "How can you call your great teacher's name directly? You should call his name respectfully as calligraphy characters Moon, then Sun, and then Myung." He taught me like that. He also said, "Since your seat seems to be uncomfortable, please change to this seat." His word and behavior were very courteous. So, it was not easy to share my opinion. Whenever I visited him, he came out wearing humble attire. He seems like a stone Buddha. Since he did not speak quickly, it took time to listen to his words. His facial expression also would not change and looked severe. He liked very much the lectures of Divine Principle and Unification Thought, and he gently asked me to come again. However, because he was worried that his request might cause me trouble, he glanced at my facial expression. Since his character was very reticent, it is difficult to know his inner situation.

I was curious how God's love is delivered to the place where Confucius lives. In the case of Buddha, God's love was delivered through someone, but with Confucius it was different. God called Confucius. When God said that he should teach God through his thought, he gave a full bow before God. Because he gave the full bow very politely, it took quite a long time. Why does God treat them differently? Buddha himself acted like God, but Confucius taught the various requirements of etiquette and norm. He did not act like God. There are many people around Confucius who look courteous, wearing the traditional dress, such as overcoat and hat. It was not easy to meet Confucius. When I went to meet him, I had to pass through many doors, like passing the 12 gates.

## MUHAMMAD (PBUH)                AUGUST 12, 1997

Muhammad (PBUH) is a little distant from God and the Holy Spirit. If this were the physical world, I could say the name of the place where he dwells, but in the spirit world, it is difficult to express. In going to meet him, I encountered many difficulties. It was difficult even to find the way to go to him. As it is on Earth, he does not want people to focus on himself, so in spirit world he dislikes being easily revealed. Therefore, the meeting place wasn't bright.

He asked, "What is your motivation for coming to meet me?" After introducing myself, I respectfully said, "Since you are the noble one whom many earthly people want to meet, I also came to see you." After thinking for a while, he began to open his mouth to speak. "My life on earth was not perfect; I made mistakes and God made me realize this by sending me here. I deeply repent that I gave God cause to worry about me. But despite that, God gave special grace by letting me stay here, so I am grateful."

He continued, "When I was staying on earth, I thought that my thought was the most systematic and detailed teaching of God. I feel very ashamed for that. I cannot lift up my head before God. However, since you have come here, please feel free to say whatever you came to say." Since then I have met him four times. The reason I met him so many times is that I wanted to understand his thought clearly. During the second meeting, I explained a part of the Unification Thought and introduced True Father, and he had a surprising comprehension of it. He has already known True Father very well. He said that he was very much looking forward to seeing the Reverend Moon in the spirit world.

When I asked why he is waiting for the True Father, he said that he already knew that True Father will establish the law of the spirit world and liberate the people of the spirit world. When I asked how he came to know that, he said that it was through attending many seminars about this that were held in the spirit world.

Muhammad (PBUH) was wearing a robe, which covered his entire body from head to foot. He had the character of religious founder, and stood as a dignified figure. Most people surrounding him were dressed similarly, such as we see in the Arab countries. People who are living in this Arab area were trying to avoid meeting others. If I tried to see them, they turned their faces. Even though I asked the reason, they didn't give me an answer. I came to guess that they feel uncomfortable around me.

Muhammad (PBUH) seemed glad to meet me, and at the same time, seemed to feel shy. He always met me bashfully. While staying here, I have never seen God call Muhammad (PBUH) or make any request of him. Even though Muhammad (PBUH) recognized God's love and felt sorry for God, I could not see that he gave a full bow and devotion as did Buddha and Confucius. However, I don't know if he is doing that when I am not there. He doesn't seem to feel lonely, as Buddha does, and he also doesn't seem to have a meek face like Confucius.

How did so great a man as the leader of Islam come to be in this situation in spirit world? I have thought deeply about that and here is my viewpoint.

Man was created to pursue goodness by loving as God

loves. However, it seems that Muhammad's successors at times pursued individual desire through autocratic authority rather than following goodness and love. The mind by which we serve God should spring automatically from the original nature. Faith produced by forcible and cruel methods is just formal faith. Moreover, forcible methods oppress the original human nature. It is far from God's way. Therefore, those who practiced it cannot but take responsibility for it in spirit world. Muhammad (PBUH) is looking forward to seeing the true God, but he is in a difficult situation. He can resolve this problem and go before God only when he has the cooperation of earthly people. Therefore, if people of his faith attend the Blessing ceremony and pray for him, he will like that very much.

## EMMANUEL SWEDENBORG    *AUGUST 13, 1997*

Swedenborg was the one whom I most wanted to meet in my earthly life. In order to meet him, I waited for God's will. What does God think of that? God said that even though man's ability is limited, the power of the Holy Spirit is infinite. Swedenborg was one who thought the power of God more preciously than human ability.

He is staying in a good place that is close to Paradise. Before I met him, I looked around at his surroundings. His disciple came out to meet me. He said, "My teacher welcomes you." He said that his teacher received the revelation that God's messenger would visit today. So, now he is waiting for you. When I entered the room, Swedenborg greeted me with a bright smile and face. It was a very good feeling.

When I sat silently to introduce myself, he said, "You are the one who received God's love and special grace and lived attending a precious teacher. Therefore, can you give me a lecture of your teacher's thought?" So, I introduced briefly about Divine Principle and Unification Thought. He also asked me to introduce True Father, who had given such precious teaching.

When I responded that he would already know about True Father, he said, "Your teacher is the one who is a luminary like the sun and the moon. Because you attended such a teacher who cannot be evaluated by human thinking, I have to learn from you." He asked me with that humble attitude. I promised him to have many chances to talk with him.

Swedenborg had a very systematic and logical thought. I was wondering why this person stays near Paradise even though he experienced God's love and was serving God. He was in the place where he could see God closely and was waiting for God's grace.

However, because he lived communicating with God for a long time, even when he came to the spirit world, his spiritual eyes shone very brightly. People who are attending him also had bright faces and humble minds. However, because they don't know True Parents' thought and the Blessing, I came to think that before True Father comes to this world, I would witness to them by giving lectures as soon as possible.

## SUNDAR SINGH                    AUGUST 13, 1997

This person is the one who saw the high-level spirit world while on earth. I could compare Swedenborg and Sundar Singh. The place where Sundar Singh is staying is located in the middle spirit world, which is lower than Paradise. Before I met him, I came across various decorations that were spread all around. It was as before a female shaman dances. The surroundings of the house were similar to the Buddhist style.

When I entered his house to meet Sundar Singh, a servant guided me, spreading salt before my way. Sundar Singh did not come out from his room, but instead someone else opened the door. When he saw me, he said, "How does such a precious person visit here?" I introduced myself in detail, and I told him that I came here in order to introduce Divine Principle, Unification Thought, and True Parents. He said that "You are very gracious to me, but I don't have any qualification and I have come to have a guilty conscience." When I asked what was the reason, he said that while he stayed in the physical world, he received not only the Holy Spirit, but also spirits from other levels. So, he feels shameful before God. He said that after giving a sacrificial offering, he would listen to my lecture.

He was very humble and silent, but he spoke very clearly and logically. However, I could not say that God would not like the decorations around his house. I think that when he receives the Divine Principle lectures, his ideas will change.

The spirit world differs according to level, and people who are close to God are more comfortable, while people who do not know about God tend to argue very much with one another and be in anguish. Although I wanted to restore this area, I do not have confidence to accomplish that even by giving dozens of Divine Principle lectures. I feel very sorry for True Parents.

## SOCRATES

Many people may think of Socrates when they are in a complicated and confused situation in their thought. Man is trying to seek God according to the original nature given at his birth. Before human beings rationally recognize the fact that they were created by God, they are in the heartistic relationship with God, which is the relationship of parent and child. Therefore, man's original mind to pursue God will necessarily seek and find God. However, if you are captured too much by your own thought, you will lose God. I think that Socrates is such a person.

In order to meet this person, I made great efforts. However, it was not easy to meet him. The place where he is staying is located in the lowest level of the middle spirit world. The reason why it was difficult to meet him is that he was not willing to meet me. When I visited there the third time, he agreed to meet me, with a dark and gloomy facial expression. The reason why he did not want to meet me is because he didn't want to discuss with people who had a philosophy different from his own. He wanted to maintain the fruit of his own thought continuously, and especially he did not feel any need to listen to another way of thought. He was very arrogant, and disliked even to talk. He was unwilling to listen my talk.

However, I began to speak about the Unification Thought step by step. While I was giving a lecture, he suddenly asked me, "Who made those ideas? Is it your thought? If it is yours, you seem to think about it very much." Therefore, I began to introduce True Father, but he had not known about True Father. After I had talked for a long time, it seemed that he opened his mind a little bit. Through him, I came to recognize that philosophical thought can be an obstacle before God. Because he was filled with his own thought and logic, it seemed to take a long time to change his thinking.

When I came again the next time and asked if he wanted to listen my lecture, he said, "Since your lecture is not necessary for me, if you came with the mind to change my thought, I can hardly welcome you."

When he has a problem, he is not willing to meet other people until it has been solved. Therefore, his surroundings are dreary and at a little distance from people. He did not try to have interest in the harmony of nature in which flowers bloom and wilt, or in the fact that man's death and life are derived from God's power, or in God's existence. Because of that, it seems it will take a long time to remove his egotism. However, I did not give up hope for him, because our thought is on a level higher than any other is. When the medium asked me if he does not know about True Father and if he knows about God well, I said, "Even though he knows about God, he does not know about True Father well, and he doesn't want to know about True Father because of his own philosophy."

## ADAM                                    AUGUST 14, 1997

Adam, the first human ancestor and the first grandfather, is a handsome-looking man with a warm personality, and he always made us feel comfortable. I was curious on what level of spirit world he was living. If I tell all the details, it will take too much time, and I will be sorry for Mrs. Lee.

Adam remained too distant from God to appear before Him. However, since his indemnity period is finished, he is now living in a good spirit world that is close to God. Adam is always afraid of coming before God, being cautious.

Adam says that his life in that realm of spirit world is a lot better than that in the Garden of Eden. Things are abundant and he can meet with many people. When he was living in the Garden of Eden, he was lonely and fearful to face God. According to Adam, he did not know that he was supposed to make Eve happy. He just thought that he was to stay with Eve in the Garden of Eden. In other words, he was not mature enough to relate to Eve as a man. He was not old enough for him to realize that Eve was to be his wife. When things went wrong with Eve, he finally realized it, but it seemed too late for him to do anything about it.

Since Adam failed to fulfill his responsibility as the first human ancestor, he suffered a lot, working hard for many thousands of years. Therefore, as a sinner, he felt tremendous guilt before God. Although he is now living near God, he still is always cautious before Him.

## EVE                                          AUGUST 19, 1997

It may sound too harsh to say that Eve is the greatest sinner in human history, but it is true that she committed a truly serious mistake. Eve is now living with Adam near God. She is always warm and thoughtful but also quite stubborn. To me, her face is not the most beautiful one, but she is very good-looking. Whenever I tried to speak to her closely, she always turned her face away. When I had another chance to see her, she again turned her face away from me or bent her head down so that she would not have eye contact with me. Therefore, it took time for me to have an opportunity to talk with her.

As we were conversing with each other, when she discovered that I was close to God, she attempted to have an open and honest dialogue with me. She started by saying, "It may not be necessary for me to talk about my fault in the past, but I would like to be honest with you. Adam and I always lived close to each other, eating together, sleeping together, etc. We were so young at that time and we did not know that we should become husband and wife. Adam always liked to have fun, running here and there. I also liked to play, but I preferred to stay in a quiet place, spending time with the creation.

Although Adam and I had some time together, since we were both busy playing separately, we did not have the opportunity to express our love for each other as a man and a woman. The being that actually opened my eyes to the opposite sex was Lucifer.

"Lucifer was always with me. He was always kind and willing to teach me everything. Sometimes he would bring things that I liked to eat. In the meantime, through Lucifer I developed a feeling towards the opposite sex. Lucifer also came to fall in love with me. At the time my relationship with Lucifer came to fruition, Adam began to notice it. But Adam did not interfere in our relationship, nor did he express his love for me. He just left me alone. Then my love for Lucifer became more passionate, and Lucifer led me well. I just could not let go of Lucifer. This lasted for quite some time. Lucifer was scared and so was I. Yet whenever Adam saw me, he ran away from me. After a while I came to realize that my deeds were wrong. One day God struck us with a terrible reproach. He said that we were no longer qualified to be with Him.

"Then I looked for Adam with a sincere heart. I desperately clung to him, appealing to him to help me. Afterwards, as was taught by Lucifer, we slept together. When I had a sexual relationship with Adam, I could not feel the same passion for Adam that I felt toward Lucifer. I came to miss Lucifer more and more. Strangely, Adam and I came to feel distant from each other. Whenever Lucifer glanced at me and tempted me, he was irresistible. Eventually I was drawn to the bosom of Lucifer and could satisfy my burning physical desire through him.

"As time passed, I could not avoid God's eyes on me. I was scared of his anger towards me. Then I went to Adam. Although I had no physical relationship with him, strangely enough I felt a sort of peace. Without knowing why, whenever I went near Lucifer, I was captured by an intolerable fear. As time passed, I came to realize that what I did with Lucifer was wrong, and I felt more guilt in front of Adam.

"Adam comforted me, but my heart was always tormented. That has been the story of my life. I felt sorry for Adam, and I am a terrible sinner who cannot even ask for forgiveness and salvation from God. As the indemnity period is over, I am elevated to this place, but I am the worst sinner."

I wondered why God called such a sinner, Eve, so quickly to be near Him. When thinking that Adam and Eve, as the first human ancestors, are the unforgivable sinners and the ones who caused the greatest pain to God, I was curious how they could be in this spiritual realm.

As human history flows, the day of joy when hell is liberated should arrive as soon as possible. Otherwise, human beings cannot be liberated from pain and suffering on earth. Now, since an indemnity condition was established on their behalf, Adam's family is finally liberated. Through the liberation of Adam's family, a foundation for all sins and crimes to be forgiven is also established. Someday, the gate to hell will be wide open, and an eternal day of liberation will come.

## NOAH                                    AUGUST 19, 1997

I came to encounter Noah, Father of Faith, who built an ark on the top of a mountain. He was residing in the upper level of the middle spirit world. He always prays, bowing down and making special conditions such as sacrificial offerings to God, with all of his heart, mind and soul. He works very hard and dresses similar to the way of a farmer who plants rice seedlings. He makes an altar to make an offering to God. Using his talent that built the ark, he thoroughly checks here and there to make sure everything is perfect. He does his very best with everything he is involved in. He does this wherever he goes, in whatever he does, not only for himself but also for others. He also encourages others to pray and makes special conditions. His facial expression shows he is very kind, good-hearted, and pure, without thinking of his own interest.

I asked him, "Did you never change your heart while building an ark for 120 years at the top of a mountain?" Noah answered, "According to the direction of God, I was building an ark. Therefore, I could not change my mind in the middle. If I changed my mind, I should have doubted whether that direction was from God. I do not recall how the time period of 120 years passed because I was totally committed to building the ark. Actually, it was fun to build it. My children and wife also helped me, but their support was not 100%. People usually seek for what is visible. They often turn their faces away from God who is invisible. So, many times they shook me while I was only focusing on building the ark. They would say, 'How can we live alone when all others die in the flood? Why would God let us live alone? Let us ask this question to God and when He gives us a clear answer, we can continue to build the ark. If God destroys all humankind, there will be no descendants. God is not so cruel as to do such things to human beings, etc.' All kinds of temptations came to me, but I did not pay attention to any of them, but only focussed on building the ark. Still, I am grateful that my wife and children did not turn away from me. While we were living on earth, the greatest joy was to attend God with all of our hearts and obey His words. That is why in a wonderful place like this, I am teaching people how to attend God in the right way. This is the most joyous time for me. It may sound rude, but may I ask how you came to be given such a great grace of the love of God? How well did you attend God when you were living on earth?"

Noah did not know about the True Parents well. I explained about them for some time. Then he was immersed in deep thought for a while until he said, "You seem to have been born at the right time." He seemed to be expressing an envious heart by saying this. When I told him that everyone can be this close to God, he replied, "I am grateful for where I am. People go to the level that corresponds to the merit they received while attending God on earth." He expressed the desire to learn more about the True Parents.

Another thing that I was interested in was the time of the flood judgment. Noah responded. "God one day gave me an urgent order: 'Noah, Noah, hurry up and get into the ark with the others.' Three days thereafter, it started to rain. From that time on, all family members began to believe in me. While we were confined for three days, everyone including the animals made such a commotion to get off the ark. At that time I depended on God only and prayed constantly. The main theme of my prayer was, Please build your nation through the flood judgment. As it started to rain, everyone inside the ark remained silent. All of my family members paid attention to every single movement of my action.

"The flood that continued for 40 days and nights was truly an astonishing tempest. Due to the heavy rain, the entire world was dark. The rain flowing in the valleys made mountains fall down, with their tree branches broken. Lightening and thunder was ceaseless. Realizing that this was truly a punishment from God, I only continued to pray. All I was wondering about was when God's indignation would be stopped. Forty days later, after the rain had stopped, God said that my faith had calmed His indignation. A ray of sunshine shone on the window of the ark, the tempest started to die down. After that, all of my family members followed my directions, depending on me. There was unity in the family. It was a happy time of our life together."

I asked, "May I ask you about the mistake made by Ham?" He replied, "That year, all of us worked very hard. Especially, the harvest for grapes was a great success. Since all of us did our best, everything was abundant and our hearts were peaceful. We were just so happy. One day, I had a glass of wine after working hard and happened to fall asleep out of fatigue. I must have been too hot from drinking the wine and without realizing it, I must have taken off all my clothes, making me naked. Usually, my second son was obedient to me. Since I was sleeping, he had the desire to make sure I was sleeping comfortably. He must have come into my room, and when seeing me sleeping naked, he must have been surprised.

"My family members who had returned from work and saw me in such a condition made a commotion about it. Especially, my wife was upset with me, asking me why I could not even take care of myself as a person who attended God. The fact that I could not do it became a great sin before God. Although I had attended God all of my life, since the flood judgment I had become arrogant rather than being humble. For this, God punished us, admonishing us. God always thinks that humility comes first." Then he added that whenever he thinks of his mistake, he always feels repentant and is unable to lift his face up before God.

Noah attended God all of his life. Thus he thought that God should be able to forgive the mistake of his son, Ham, but He would not. That was because of the Fall of man, for if God forgave, it could be another condition for Satan to invade. That is why God would not forgive Ham's act. This is the law of the spirit world. There is no exception in the Heavenly law. Therefore, those who want to be treated generously before God should live a life that can pass the Heavenly law in the spirit world. Then you can be recognized and dealt with by God accordingly. I sincerely hope that people on earth will be able to come to God by passing all of His tests.

## ABRAHAM AND ISAAC                    AUGUST 20, 1997

I think I was introduced to Abraham and Isaac even before I went to meet them. I had heard, while in the spirit world, that Abraham had been meeting important figures in God's providence. They came to visit me, saying that they could not have someone important as I to come to them. Abraham is a good-looking and gentle-hearted person. When I said that I would like to go and visit his place, he answered that people around him are able to attend God well, bowing down to God in the morning and in the evening, according to the Heavenly law.

As I expressed my interest in the burnt offering of Isaac, he understood me, agreeing with me. He stated, "Since I did not have a child for a long time, I made special efforts in attending God. There was nothing that I could reject or deny in God's voice. Further, my wish was that I depend on God in everything and live with Him. As I made special efforts every day, at my age of 100 He gave me a son. The preciousness of this son was indescribable. I was so immersed in enjoying him, almost forgetting to make offerings to God, although God is the one who had given me that son.

"As the child was growing, he was interested in everything that I, his father, was doing. He loved me very much. Perhaps, it is because he is a son who was given to me after my making many special conditions for God. He would say, 'Father, today, why is there no water on the altar? God should be upset with this, and I will bring some water for Him.' In such a way he grew and grew in health and wisdom. One day, God called me and said, 'Abraham, I would like to receive an offering from you, which may be a difficult offering for you to make. Will you still do it for me?' I replied, 'I will do whatever you ask me to do. Please go ahead and tell me what to do.' Then God said, 'Abraham, I would like to have you offer your precious son, Isaac.' I thought I misheard Him and asked Him again, 'What have you said?' He answered, 'I told you to offer your son.'

I could not tolerate the pain. Whether it was day or night, everything seemed so dark to me. For several days, I was in torment. Then Isaac came to me and asked, insisting on my answering him, 'Father, is anything wrong?' I told him, 'God has asked me to make an offering.' Isaac was surprised and asked, wondering, 'Father, why are you taking so long to execute God's direction? Please do it quickly.' With his push I told him, 'I should make this offering not here, but at a place far away, in a deep mountain.' Isaac said, 'Then it is all the more reason why you should be in a hurry. Let us leave quickly.' Owing to his pressure, I could no longer resist him. Several days after our departure, when we arrived at a mountain, he asked me, 'Father, what will be the sacrificial offering object this time?' I could not answer him. As firewood was piled up, I just called Isaac's name and embraced him. Then Isaac said, 'Father, God asked you to offer Him Isaac, right? I knew it when I saw your gloomy face.' Then he continued, 'I am grateful for God to choose me as the offering object. Father, what are you worried about? Becoming an offering object is good. It is a blessing.' Then he lay down on the firewood without hesitation. Looking at the sky, I earnestly prayed with mixed feelings in my heart and with fear towards God and grief for my son, 'Father, I am offering my son to you!' With this prayer, as I was about to strike Isaac with a sword, I heard a voice from the sky, 'Abraham, I now know that you respect me. Stop what you are going to do.' Then Isaac, who was lying on the firewood sat up and pushed me, asking, 'Why are you stopping? Please continue to make the offering!' He continued, crying out loud, 'Father, if you falsely swear before God, I cannot look at your face.' Then God called, 'Isaac!' Isaac who heard His voice this time listened to me. Through this, although I had failed in making the burnt offerings according to God's direction, God forgave us, both father and son. At that time Isaac joked, 'Perhaps God thought that I was too young to be an offering object.' "

Isaac has a small build, but he is taking after his father; he is a good-looking man with a humble heart. Abraham and Isaac were close to each other to the extent that I was envious of their relationship. Abraham's offering of Isaac teaches us many lessons.

## JUDAS ISCARIOT            AUGUST 20, 1997

Judas Iscariot always ran away whenever I saw him. I went to visit him a number of times, but he would not want to see me. So one day, I left a message on a piece of paper, "Your past fault should not be hidden, but should be revealed in order to be forgiven." I again visited him several days afterwards, at which time he agreed to see me, and bending his head down like a sinner, he asked me, "Why are you coming after me who is such a great sinner?" I did not answer immediately. After some time, Judas continued, "A historical criminal like me cannot come to God or to the Lord. As I am repenting about my sin living here like this, please do not come to see me anymore."

"How painful your heart must be. It may not be a great comfort to you, but I thought I might be able to ease your painful heart," I said. He responded, "So far, there has not been even one single person who tried to comfort a sinner such as I. But no one and nothing can be a comfort to me, and therefore I again request you not to visit me anymore." I could not introduce either the Divine Principle or Unification Thought to him. His living environment was barren, like that of a prison, and I could hardly see anyone around him. Earthly people usually think that hell is a place where many people are crying and screaming, filled with an unbearable bad odor, but actually, hell is a lonely place. I returned to my place thinking that I would visit him again and help him after a while, when he is calmer.

## JOHN THE BAPTIST                    *AUGUST 20, 1997*

John the Baptist is short but has a smart-looking face. When I asked Jesus how John the Baptist was doing, Jesus asked me not to say that I had met him. He also added that John the Baptist would not want to meet me, and so I would not be able to meet him. The place of John the Baptist was very distant from that of Jesus. When I went to visit him, a gigantic person who was carrying a sword stopped me, saying that not everyone was allowed to see his master. Then he asked me to put down my name in the visitors' book. As I entered his house after signing my name, John the Baptist received me, bowing down and said, "How could the messenger of God come to such a humble place as mine," and he sat down, kneeling down before me. Even before I asked him any questions, he started to talk. "On earth, I was respected and followed by many people, but now, my dwelling place is so humble and I cannot even see the Lord. Further, even if I would like to attend the Lord, He would not come here. I was so accustomed to be attended and I did not pay attention to Jesus' life at all. Because I thought and related to Jesus not with God's eyes, but with human eyes... I did not realize that it would be such a great sin. Since I do not know how to be forgiven, I am frustrated. As you came here as the messenger of God, could you help me?"

When I asked him why a man with a sword was guarding the gate, he answered that he is always insecure with a fear that someone might come to hurt him and therefore he meets people selectively. I told him, "You need to continuously repent until the day when the gates of hell will be opened," and I introduced True Parents to him. Then he asked me when that day of liberation will come. As I was returning home, my heart ached because I know that before True Parents there are many people like him on earth, who will be living a life like that of John the Baptist in the spirit world.

## KIM, IL SUNG                          AUGUST 21, 1997

To meet him I had to go everywhere to look for him. I asked God about his whereabouts but God only shook his head. I asked around but nobody knew. So I finally decided to go down to low levels to look for him. When I went down to a low level, I really felt that there is hell. Then what happened? A giant man injured by gun and knife was leaning against the door, not able even to go inside, and sat there, such a ghastly sight. I asked him, "By any chance are you the Premier IL Sung Kim?" He was moaning and groaning and could not even hold his head up, and asked who I was. I told him who I am and mentioned Father's name.

He was bleeding everywhere but he changed his position to kneel down. He said, "I committed so much sin, and did so many wrong things to him; therefore I am paying for all that now." I asked him, "Why don't you go inside instead of staying here by the entrance?" He said, "I wish I could do that, but as soon as I go in, those people throws stones, knives, guns, and all kinds of things at me and create such a riot that I cannot endure. Also they scream and say, 'Go away, you son of a bitch,'—so I cannot stay inside.

"Why are you looking for me? Do you think that my son Jung Il would know about all my misery? North Korea will perish. I knew that already, but I could not do anything about it. I was just hoping that Jung Il would attend True Father and listen his advice to lead the country. I never knew that the North Korean people's shouting and screaming was as loud as this. I really did not know my sin was so great like this. Nobody welcomes me anywhere. Could you please save me?" he begged. I had to give Divine Principle and Unification Ideology lectures, but I really could not bear to see that gruesome scene. I went inside the door; it was like the open space of a jail. All the people who were there rose and asked me, "Who are you? How could you come in here so imposingly?" I told them that I am a messenger from God and requested a little bit of time to talk.

From here and there, I heard people saying sarcastically, "All right. We have plenty of time. Give us a speech." I explained to them that God is the central person of love, and after that gave a lecture about the dual characteristics of God. I also appealed to them with tears for about 40 to 50 minutes that they should live for others, love and help each other and forgive each other's fault. They must endure and wait until the day of liberation of hell.

After that, I told Il Sung Kim to lie down for treatment of his wounds. People around us started to help by cleaning his wounds, and the atmosphere changed to very calm and composed. I asked to come again later on for more lectures. Some said that would be fine and some said to let it be and did not want to be bothered.

Il Sung Kim sat down anxiously. He could not lift his head up and he could not even look at me when I was leaving. On the way back I was thinking that earthly life is so short. Who can know about this kind of fact? Earthly people cannot see the Spirit World; therefore, they only cling to what they can see and live their lives. This kind of punishment of hell, the life that can only face this kind of wretched hell: What a poor life! I am writing this letter in the hope of being a vital energy for our members so that without suffering, all of our members can be directly embraced into God's bosom.

## REALM OF UNIFICATION
## SPIRIT WORLD                          *AUGUST 21, 1997*

I'll explain the realm of Unification Spirit World. Here is a real heaven. Here is a real Eden. Here is real peace. Here, everybody is happy. Here is full of hope. Here is a real garden of love. Here is real rapture. Here is a place that really sprouts a bud of love. Here is a holy place of beauty that cannot be adequately expressed. Here Heung Jin Nim is always the first to do the work very quietly, humbly and with great detail. He always asks God about the work and seeks His opinion. He goes around each level, and listens to people's situations and comforts them and so on. Missionary Chong Goo Park always attends Heung Jin Nim and goes everywhere with him. Sometimes Missionary Park stops Heung Jin Nim from going to very difficult places and he takes care of things instead of Heung Jin Nim.

Dae Mo Nim always prays, just as she had done during her earthly life. She does not move from Heung Jin Nim's living place, and she always prays. Dae Mo Nim lives with only one mind and wish, which is long life for the True Parents. Choong Mo Nim calls Dae Mo Nim elder mother, and she always follows next to Dae Mo Nim and tries to learn even all the little things. One time I witnessed a very interesting scene. Dae Mo Nim's couple and Choong Mo Nim's couple were together and talking to each other, and Dae Mo Nim's husband said, "Let's have a fun time together. I feel we are so distant because we are too serious and too formal with each other." Then Dae Mo Nim said, "How can in-laws have fun time together? Aren't in-laws supposed to be formal and serious to each other?" After that the atmosphere changed to serious again. Choong Mo Nim is always serious and formal, and she tries very hard to learn.

President Hyo Won Eu always gives Divine Principle lectures. He returns to the lecturing position even when talking with members comfortably. Divine Principle lecturing is his life itself. Even in this kind of happy atmosphere, we have some bad times also. Many of our members are here, but that doesn't mean that everybody is happy. They carry the title of their sins like carrying a name-tag so it is publicly revealed. Therefore, until they pay off the indemnity, they face many embarrassments and pains.

Even in heaven, there are different levels. I am not going to say any more about it. But if I summarize it, Heavenly life is the extension of earthly life. The Spirit World is like going in to the storage with the fruit of your own life. But more precious than grain is the attitude of living for the sake of others. We all learned about give and take action from the Divine Principle, and the very basis of that is living for the sake of others. Therefore, if we live for others rather than ourselves, it will be all right.

# CHAPTER FIVE

# MEETINGS IN THE SPIRIT WORLD II

# LEADERS OF THE COMMUNIST WORLD

## KARL MARX                                    MAY 19, 1998

Karl Marx lived his earthly life as the chief of evil persons. Why was he so ruthless? His rebelliousness derived from his resentment over the lack of recognition he received for what he considered his great and wonderful ideas. He was not willing to open his mind to discussion because of his awful pride and arrogance over his thought. Thus, he rebelled against the social system and his thought provided the raging mob with the foundation for their revolution. I wondered where such a ruthless person, who was intoxicated with his own ideas during his lifetime, would live in the spirit world.

It was not easy to find him at first. But then I realized that those of the same kind flock together, so in order to find him, I asked here and there for where revolutionaries are to be found.

People who worked for revolution on earth still are intoxicated with themselves in the spirit world. Around the place where Karl Marx lives there I found shabby buildings that look like detainment centers for prisoners of war. In those houses, there were many people who look like remnants of a defeated army. They were exhausted persons who were laying down because they have nothing to do, and disabled persons who walked leaning on crutches. Their faces were spiritless, reflecting the miserable realities of war. Nevertheless, they were going somewhere. They followed a guide.

Then I heard someone shouting with a loud voice from a high place. "My fellow citizens!" he shouted, "Let's start again! We cannot be defeated here. Let's encourage each other and struggle once again! Victory is ours." He was shouting that sort of rhetoric. The man shouting was the very Karl Marx.

I waited to meet him at the rear of the audience. Regardless of the people's difficulties, he continuously insisted that his theory would bring victory. After his speech, I asked him to meet me for a moment in spite of his busy schedule. When I asked, he said to me, "What kind of thought do you represent?" Then I introduced myself, "I am Sang Hun Lee, and I systematized the Critique and Counterproposal to Communism." He replied, "I have nothing to do with the Critique and Counterproposal to Communism. I have no time to talk with you because I am very busy." When he said this, I responded, "No matter how busy you are, you should not treat me like that. I waited for you until your lecture was finished." He lowered his eyes at that, and asked me to sit down with him. He would not let me say even one word. Fortunately, I was willing to listen to him as he explained his theories.

He was a great theorist. He talked about his theory without stopping for breath. Because he strongly insisted on his opinion, I could not open the door of dialogue. I waited continuously. When he seemed to be ready to finish talking, I stood up and said that it was my turn. I said, "I, Sang Hun Lee, am a person who likes to listen to others, but since you have finished speaking, I would like to offer my opinion." I then talked about the core contents of the Critique and Counterproposal to Communism. I explained why the theory of communism failed of necessity.

"Even though your theory is very great," I concluded,

"because it explains nothing about God, who exists as a reality in human life on earth and in heaven, communism could not but fail. Do you know God? Without knowing God, you cannot teach about the fundamental purpose of human life. Without knowing God, there is no peace and eternal life for human beings. There is only war. Aren't these all the people who were intoxicated with your thought? Let's look at them! Why do they all live like defeated and failed people?

"Please follow me. Let's go to where I live and look around that place. Let's talk continuously on the way. I would like to invite you to my house today. Please let's go."

When I said this, it seemed that I hurt his pride. So I talked to him very politely. "I would like to invite you as a guest at my house. I want to treat you with great respect." He seemed to feel a sense of obligation to follow me.

While we were on the way, he asked me, "Why did you come here? Why did you come to me and give me an enthusiastic lecture?" I answered, "You will find out when you come to my house." When we arrived, he looked around the beautiful and fantastic natural environment where I live. He seemed to feel very sad. I guided him to various places and showed him one special place. I showed him a beautiful vista of a couple loving each other. Marx was not surprised or embarrassed, on the contrary he was attracted by it; he seemed to be drawn to them by magnetic attraction. Moreover, on the street, people's bright and peaceful facial expressions seemed to cause his thinking to change.

He asked me if there were more places I could show him. I answered, "How can you see everything in a day? I will guide you to more places next time." He asked again whether he could live there. His attitude had changed very much after seeing this world. I came to think that there was a good chance to speak to him about God. When I said "Only people who adore and worship God can live here," he said, "Let's go to God." When I answered, "God is not here," he said "Then I will go to God and ask some questions. What shall I do in order to adore God? If God gives me some guidance, I will do exactly what He says." Since Karl Marx's mind had opened slightly, I began to give him a Divine Principle lecture, pointing out the errors of his thought. While I was giving the lecture, I could discern from his facial expression that he was in anguish over the difference between what I was teaching and his thought. However, I lectured without stopping.

In this way, I lectured him so many times. One day during my lecture, I suggested that we would have more lectures at his house. He said that he needed more time before inviting me to his house. However, by the time I finished the lecture, he said, "Because today's lecture was more interesting than yesterday's, tomorrow's will likely be more interesting than today's, and the day after tomorrow's more than tomorrow's. So I suggest that I invite you to my house when all lectures are finished."

In response, I said to him, "Because it takes much time to finish all my lectures, let's stop this lecture right now. Then, when your mind really wants to listen to the lectures again, let's begin again." My intention was to be able to give the lectures in his home. When I suggested, "Because your house is too small, so let us do the lecture in your big yard," his face became cool, and he said, "I know the reason you want give an enthusiastic lecture there. Anyway, let's have the lecture there."

One day during my lecture, some strange young people entered the room and asked Marx, "Why do you listen to the lecture all by yourself?" They said that they wanted to listen also. I thought that it was a good chance and invited them to come into the room. From here and there, many people gathered. Then a strange thing happened. Marx's face turned as red as a beet. He began to cry with his head down in front of the entire audience. He continued to cry, and then spoke, "My friends who have gathered here! Please listen to this teacher's lecture." He guided all the people to an open place. In this way, in a wide-open yard, I came to be able to give various lectures in the Divine Principle and Critique and Counterproposal to Communism to many people. Through my lecture, 70-80 % of Marx's followers came to be favorable. Marx was disappointed about that.

At this time he is very close to me, but he has not reached the point of accepting True Parents. However, since he is listening to my lectures very carefully and positively, I believe that he will accept True Parents soon. I will explain to him that the messianic thought of True Parents is the completion of all systems of thought.

## LENIN

As the leading figure of the communist revolution, Lenin may have been a contributor to communist countries, but is the lowest person before God. Where does he live in the spirit world? I have been to his house before. I went there in order to discuss the Critique and Counterproposal to Communism with him.

When I entered his house, there were many security guards and they checked everything. So it was hard to go into his house. I introduced myself proudly as God's emissary. The procedure to gain an appointment was complicated, and because the purpose for the visit was unfamiliar, it was not easy to gain entrance. Because I could not wait any longer, I told them again that I came as God's emissary with an invitation for their teacher. I told them, "I am going to attend your teacher very well, so please let me go inside." Finally I could pass through.

Lenin was not so big or tall, but his face was very handsome and made an impression of strength. He asked me, "What are you going to accomplish by meeting me?" I answered, "Originally, I had great interest in your thought. I want to meet you and learn your theory directly from you." Lenin did not easily reveal his mind and thinking. He said, "I am not so benevolent that I would speak unguardedly about my thought to a person unknown to me." He tried to verify my identity. When I introduced myself as a physician, he responded, "Why does a doctor such as you care about the disposition of revolutionary?" His mind was not open enough to allow us to discuss our thinking with each other. So I told him, "Because you are a very valuable and important person, I am grateful to meet you. I would like to invite you to my house." He expressed his deep appreciation for me very politely. So, I told him that I would come back to bring him on the next day.

The next day, I did not enter his house and instead I sent one person to call on him. Then a strange thing happened. Lenin had disappeared, although he had promised clearly to meet me. I asked those in attendance when he would come back, but no one knew. My planning was in vain. Every house around there looked very gloomy and shabby. Those poor-looking houses stood very close to one another. Why was he unwilling to meet me? I considered various reasons. For the next two days, I explored around his house. As I walked, I tried to come up with some inspiration or wisdom.

After a few days, I discovered a new house among the many houses in Lenin's neighborhood. It was no bigger than

Lenin's was. Lenin and a group emerged from this house. However, I could pick up that they considered it to be an uncomfortable or strange situation. Lenin did not display his audacious and strong features. He seemed to be tense and afraid something. What is the reason for that? I tried to come up with the reason. In any case, the company came out of the house and did not go to Lenin's house, but in a different direction. I followed them, sometimes at a distance and sometimes very closely. As I did so, I witnessed another situation. Lenin's facial expression reflected that he felt oppressed by someone. The group scattered and began to walk separately. I did not want to lose them so I chased them very carefully. They arrived at an intermediary point and began walking together again. I was wondering what their final destination would be. It turned out to be a little stream.

There they sat down side by side. Because I had to listen what they were saying, I went into the water off a little ways and pretended to wash my feet. I could hear what they were saying. I heard Lenin's voice. "My friends!" he said, "We have to fight here and gain victory. Otherwise, all of us will be expelled. A dangerous circumstance is coming." I heard the voice of a young man. "Even though we are united into one, because we don't have many members, I think it will be difficult to win." After that young man's voice, the group was silent for a while. And then, Lenin's voice was heard again. "If our identity is known to others, we will be in danger. Therefore, let's move to another place and stay there! If we move to a small house, we will be safer." I was wondering why they had come there, and why they had to talk secretly. But my question was answered soon.

If they had met in their residence, they would have been watched under close guard. I recognized from their dialogue that in their residence, because they watch one another, they cannot divulge any secrets.

Because Lenin followed a mistaken theory, even though he was a great leader in one nation, his life's results were miserable. Therefore he could not speak even a word with dignity, and he did not have a comfortable place in which to live. If he lived with splendor in the eternal world, he would be able to walk with confidence, raising his head. However, he has to live a limited life, always looking over his shoulder. Lenin's situation provides real instruction for people on earth. How should we live in order to prepare for eternal life?

I returned home praying that I can meet Lenin again in the near future.

Question (Young Soon): "In the physical world, you drove a car. Do you walk to witness people in the spirit world?"

Answer (Sang Hun Lee): "Because it is difficult to understand life in the spirit world, even though I explain it, you may not understand much. However, I will try. When one walks on earth to get somewhere, you have to walk continuously, but in the spirit world, since location changes according to one's thinking, walking has a different meaning. One can ride a car wherever and whenever one desires it. This is little bit difficult to explain. Even though you may want to know in greater detail, I will stop here and turn to the next task.

## STALIN

When God created this world, He restricted the capacity of the human brain and reason. But, Stalin lived his earthly life exercising his authority as if he were God. He wanted to surpass his restricted status as God's creature.

It was not difficult to find Stalin. I thought that Stalin would live near Karl Marx. At a place far away from Stalin's house, many people often gather together. Stalin attends the meeting and proudly tries to show off his authority as he did on the earth. The houses that are around Stalin look like the small houses made of mud, surrounded by fence, which we can see in North Korea. The people in them live poor lives. All of them on earth had served Stalin as God. Around that area are desolate and lonely surroundings. There is a horrible atmosphere that makes you feel as if someone is likely to suddenly jump at you. You always feels as if you are being watched. How is Stalin treated? Because he lived like a king on the earth, do the people serve him as if he is a king in the spirit world?

After watching the surroundings silently for a few days, a person opened the door of his room and called for someone to come. He was calling for Stalin. I was anxious about the reason Stalin has to hide and enter the room secretly. As I watched, a man and a woman entered the room, all the while looking around fearfully. Then I waited for long time, and no one came out or went into the room. I changed into shabby clothes and approached the house. I expected that they would discover me, and I was planning to say, "I came to beg for some food." I went to the door and listened, and heard a voice say, "I cannot endure my brethren shedding blood any longer. Let us go back to our families and have a comfortable lives!" I waited and listened.

Then I heard Stalin's voice. "Before coming here," he said, "I fought so many times for the sake of my nation and brethren. In light of that, how can we be defeated? You misunderstand about our situation. If we are united into one, we can gain victory." Then a woman shouted out, "Dear king, Stalin! You gave us nothing except suffering and tears. We cannot follow you or serve you any more." After she spoke, she began to cry.

Why could they possibly be here? Because most of the people here are those who protested against Stalin's autocracy, if Stalin's followers apprehend them, their families have no way to be saved. Therefore, they meet secretly avoiding observation. However, what is Stalin doing? Why does he work secretly? It was very difficult to figure out his identity just by observation.

One day I was able to go into his house wearing a mask. When I said, "I came here to meet the great teacher," a young man came out of the entrance and asked, "Where are you from? Who are you?" I said, "I heard that the teacher whom I desired to meet stays here, so I came here to receive his teaching." I waited for a while, but Stalin did not come out. Instead, another young man came out and said "Our teacher will not go to the place where people do not honor him as king." However, at a moment, a strange thing happened. I was facing the front gate and Stalin suddenly appeared behind me. As I tried to turn around and look at him, some young men suddenly appeared and grasped me tightly, shouting "How dare you come here?" I quickly said to them, "I came here to meet my respectable teacher. What is wrong with that?" They said, "Show us your identity!"

I, Sang Hun Lee, shouted out with strong confidence in God, "I am God's emissary, sent by God. God called me to you." Stalin said, "Where is God? If you bring God here, I will visit Him." When I said, "God does not have the leisure to visit an individual family," Stalin replied, "I also have no spare time. I am very busy." However, the young men were not willing to release me. So I politely said to them, "What if I study your teacher's theory right here?" Soon they released me.

Stalin asked me, "What do you want to know?" Because I had much interest in his thought anyway, I answered, "I want to learn your thought." He said, "Then let's begin tomorrow." I countered, "Because I am here anyway, I want to learn something from you today." He suggested that we meet at another place, because the place we were in was not a proper one to discuss theoretical matters. Finally I promised him to meet the next day and departed. However, when I tried to exit the way I had come in, the young men held me and threatened that if I returned, I would confront serious danger.

The next day, I met Stalin at a dark and gloomy place a little ways away from that place. He was the only one there. When I asked, "Why are you alone, even though you are a great man?" he didn't say anything. He just led me to a small quiet room. That room was a secret place that Stalin uses. He asked me, "Do you really want to learn my theory?" I answered in the affirmative, but he said that his feeling was not so good and that he would not be able to give his lecture with much enthusiasm. He said, "Because I live in seclusion, if I speak about my theory publicly, I will be expelled from this place. Not many people around here know who I am. So I'm wondering how you knew me." I said, "Because I work as God's messenger, I have the means to know." When I said that, he replied that if I would provide him a place to hide, he would be willing to follow me.

I immediately realized that I had a good chance to open his mind, so I suggested that he come to my house and teach me his theory there. When I said this, his face was overcome with fear. His eyes and entire attitude seemed to reflect his fear that I would torture him. Nonetheless, he asked me to show him the way of salvation. When I responded, "Rather, I would have you save me," he said, "All right; I will follow you."

That very day, I guided Stalin and showed him all around where I live. He saw all varieties of peaceful and comfortable life, beautiful dance and song, the beauty of all things of creation, and the splendor of God. He asked me what kinds of people are those who live here. I said that only people who served God and attended him can live here. Like Karl Marx, he also said, "Where is God? Please guide me to Him. I am going to serve and attend Him." When I said that only after studying Unification Thought completely, can you receive permission to meet God, he urged me to quickly begin his course of study in Unification Thought. I explained about Unification Thought, the Critique and Counterproposal to Communism, and the thought of True Parents, and pointed out in detail the errors of Communism. After listening to my lecture, he asked, "Where did you learn this?" I replied that I learned it from the True Parents when I lived in the physical world. So, he said, "Your parent is very great person and great revolutionary." When I taught him that my parent is revolutionary, but he is a revolutionary of true love and the savior of all humankind, he said, "When I was in the physical world, I also was treated like a savior." I asked, "Then why do you live a life of seclusion now?" He answered, "Because people do not treat me well."

He did not yet recognize that his theory was wrong. It seems that I must take a great deal of time in order to persuade him. He seems to need time to receive True Parents. However, as long as he pays attention on my lectures, I believe that there is hope.

True Father and Mother! Please wait for the day of victory. I, Sang Hun Lee, will reach the enemy of True Parents.

Question (Young Soon Kim): "Stalin killed more people than Hitler. Nonetheless, Stalin just lives a life of seclusion. Why?"

Answer (Sang Hun Lee): "Mrs. Kim! If one commits sin and lives in hiding, is it happy life? It may be a life of even greater suffering. When one lives in hiding, his is a life filled with fear."

## II. THE WORLD WAR CRIMINALS

### HITLER                                                    MAY 20, 1998

Hitler killed Jews with great cruelty. Of all the murderers of history, Hitler inflicted the cruelest slaughter. I thought that he would live among an evil group. I was very busy finding people whom I wanted to meet. In the course of my efforts, I happened to hear a group of Jews shouting, "Let's kill him." When I turned my head and looked, I witnessed a tremendous mass of people, all of whom were bound in chains, shouting, "Kill him! Kill him!" The crowd was so vast I could not see its end. Further, I could not readily find out who it was whom the crowd wanted to kill. The shouting of the crowd continued. There were many people covered with blood. Some of them fell down and were dragged on by others. It was a tragic scene reminiscent of a battlefield. Still I could not discover the object of their murderous wrath. Searching here and there, I tried to find that unfortunate person. In my heart, I felt as if I was digging up mines in a minefield.

Oh my! What's wrong here? There came into my view someone hanging on a tree, his body naked. Because he was in the middle of the mass of people, I could not see him well. No one seemed to regard this naked man as human. They shouted, "You should suffer more than you made us suffer. Do you feel shameful? Women! Please hold and touch this guy's testicles. How attractive the balls of that person are! He slaughtered millions of people as if they were animals. Touch the letters that are written on his chest. What do the letters say? Are you the King of the Nazis? Because you exercised a king's authority over us, now we will judge you as a people judge their evil king." They shouted all varieties of curses and insulting language at him. "Pull out his eyes. Pull out his hair. Light his hair on fire." All this and more and more. No matter how miserable a man's life can be on the earth, no scene that horrible could possible take place on earth.

If I had tried to help him, I am sure his tormentors would have killed me. But in view of such a tragic scene, it was heart wrenching to depart without doing anything. After returning home, I could not endure the pain in my heart. Whom should I ask to repent first? Whom should I embrace; to whom should I teach about God and talk about True Parents? I could not resolve this question. So, I prayed to God.

"Heavenly Father!" I cried in prayer, "What can I do for the poor people who are suffering in such agony?" I prayed sincerely for God's answer. At that moment, I heard God's voice. "Sang Hun-ah! I understand what you are going through. However, since those people are suffering in painful resentment (han), until their anguish is released, you have to wait. If you ask them to pardon Hitler now, they will kill you. Please wait. Hitler has to pay indemnity for the evil he committed during his earthly life. When one commits sin, one must pay indemnity. Whenever you pass by that place, your heart will be painful. At that time, please pray for him and offer consolation. How much han can they have? As time passes, they will become calm." This was God's word.

I prepared various lectures in order to dialogue with Hitler. But, whenever I went to that place, the same awful events were taking place. When one group of people shouted so much that they became exhausted, another group came and repeated the same thing. One day, I went into the crowd and met a young woman. She was slender and quite pretty. When I asked her how she was killed, she turned her head and asked me not to bring that up. So I approached the subject with the heart that God had conveyed. "How unfairly you have been treated! How much pain you must have in your heart! I can understand your painful heart." This moved her mind. She said that she was murdered as we see that person being murdered. What she meant was that she was naked when she was killed, and soldiers came and looked at her as much as they wanted. They put her into the gas chamber and whenever they wanted to look at her, they opened the door and looked at her until she became unspeakably miserable. And then, finally, they released the poison gas that killed her.

The naked Hitler is the object of all this resentment. Even though he is completely exhausted as a result of the vengeful shouting, he is forced to endure it continuously. You in the physical world cannot imagine how miserable he is.

I met another person whose hands and feet were bound in chains. I tried to console him, saying, "How much suffering are you going through? How much pain do you feel?" He said, "That person confined us and made us live according to his will. Therefore, we lived in captivity, and because that person regarded our tribe as his enemy, we could not survive. We cannot even imagine his cruelty. Now, our tribe is going to get revenge. If we collect all the chains that bound us, and cover him with them, it will be his gigantic tomb. I believe that our wish will be absolutely be realized some day. We all want to grind up him, mix his dust with water and drink it. And even if we are can do that, still our resentment will remain." That was how that one man expressed his resentment.

How can I fully describe this miserable and tragic scene in

words? It is constant suffering and continuous agony in end-less repetition. However, I have to love those poor people. So, I will wait little while longer and visit them again. In order to meet Hitler, I have to wait until the situation around him becomes calm. I am waiting in prayer and meditation upon God's word. I hope that I can meet him as soon as possible.

## MUSSOLINI

There are many things that people need in order to carry on their lives. Food, shelter and clothing are particularly essential. Mussolini's idea was that weapons are the most important thing for a person to have in life. He was absolutely convinced that a person with a large store of weapons could devour all the countries around him, and achieve victory in every situation. The most wicked aspect of his thought was that killing was not a sin. He believed that people were justified to dispose of people who got in the way, because this was no different than what was practiced in the animal world. I was curious to know about this person's life, his thoughts and about his life in the spiritual world.

Whereas Stalin's life can be described as a continuation of a secluded existence, Mussolini can be described as leading the ideal of a secluded existence. Simply put, he may be in one place today but a completely different place tomorrow. He has no permanent habitat of his own, and must wander from place to place like a gypsy. You may wonder how I came to meet Mussolini. He has no place of his own but is always making himself a burden on others, so I happen to meet him while I was visiting someone else.

The people in that area told me, "That person over there doesn't have a home. He's always wondering from place to place. He could stay with us if he wanted, but in a little while he will leave." I was curious to find out who this person was and why he lived like this.

One day, I followed this man as he went along, hoping to discover his identity. I was very careful not to let him know that he was being followed. He stopped at three or four places, but he never engaged anyone in serious conversation. Instead, he would just exchange a few words and then move on. Then one day, Lee Sang-hun grabbed hold of this man and shouted: "Brother! Let's talk for a while." He acted very surprised, and demanded to know who I was. I told him that if he didn't have a home, we could go to my home. I told him we wouldn't be disturbed there. There would be only the sound of elegant music, and there would be many places where we could have a very wonderful conversation, I said. He replied, though, that wandering from place to place was suited to his character and he didn't want to settle down anywhere. So, I asked him if we could at least be friends. He wanted to know who I was, so I said that I, too, didn't have a permanent home. I said I had a place where I could stay, but I wasn't comfortable there, so I was wandering around. I suggested that we travel together as friends, since two would surely be better tan one. He cocked his head in a gesture of bewilderment. I decided that I would travel along with him until I could find out his identity.

I'm not sure how many days passed. He asked me what I had done in the physical world. I told him that I was originally a doctor of internal medicine. Then, I asked him what he had done in the physical world. That's when he started to open up.

"I was a major leader of a certain country," he told me. "I had always had a keen interest in international affairs, and at some point I began to have a growing feeling of ambition.

Soon, I began to have a desire to become a figure of worldwide caliber, and so I focused the entire economy on building up the military arsenal. What I am today is a result of my thirst for power while I was on earth. My name is Mussolini. I am a monstrous criminal. Because I am a criminal, wherever I go I am always afraid that someone might recognize me. That's why I am always trying to hide. My heart is very much at ease now, because I have opened up to you. Why is it that you are following me around?"

I replied, "I was hoping to find you. I will tell you much more about that later. How would you like to hear me give a lecture?"

He said he was quite willing to listen, but that he was afraid that if he stayed anywhere for an extended period, people would discover his identity. "If that happens, then not only will I be caste out again but I will also be cursed," he said.

I told him, "If someone commits a crime, then it's natural that he be punished. Also, I think a person has to know and understand the seriousness of the crime he committed and then never repeat his crime. If you've done something wrong, then of course you have to face punishment. How long do you intend to keep running away?" I tried to explain this to him in a way that he would understand.

As it turned out, the good in Mussolini's character outweighed his temperament as a thief to a greater extent than I had expected. When I pointed out the errors in his ways, he responded with gratitude. Also, he asked me politely to let him hear my lecture. Since he didn't have a home where we could go, I asked him where he wanted me to give the lecture. He responded that he would follow the lead of his "teacher." So, I decided to open up my home to him. It seems, though, that this person led a very complex life in the bedroom – that is, his relationship with women. When he saw my bedroom, he asked how it was that I could have such a good and beautiful room, but have only one woman. I was at a loss to know where I should begin with this person. At any rate, we settled ourselves in my home.

First, I explained to him the motivation for the fall. He asked a lot of questions. He wanted to know where I had learned this, what grounds I had for believing this, and so on. Methodically, I took him step by step through the Principle lecture, Victory Over Communism Thought, Unification Thought, explaining everything in detail. He was deeply impressed with the content. He asked me many questions — "Who taught this to you? Who came up with these ideas? How did he figure all this out?" The heartistic distance between us, though, was too great for me to give him the answers to these questions in much detail. I simply told him that I had learned these things during my time on earth from the Rev. Sun Myung Moon, who is the True Parents. Mussolini then remarked that Rev. Moon's theories were very systematic, but that it would be very difficult for someone to actually live according to these ideas.

As a final matter, Mussolini needed a place to stay. I asked him how long he expected to keep wandering around. He told me he hadn't made up his mind on any particular place yet, and that he would decide on a place when he found some place that was appropriate. It is God's Will. As yet, he doesn't understand the conditions for indemnity or the root of evil, so it is likely to take considerable time. I can only give praise to True Parents and pray that God will help him.

Question: Dr. Lee, what language did you use when talking to these people? Confucius spoke Chinese, Shakyamuni spoke the language of India, Jesus spoke Aramaic, Karl Marx spoke German, Hitler spoke German, Mussolini spoke Italian.

Answer: In the spiritual world, I meet someone and my meaning is conveyed to that person. Then, that person's meaning is conveyed to me, so there is no need for language. When I look at a person, my meaning is conveyed to him. When he looks at me, his meaning is conveyed to me.

## TOJO                                                    *MAY 21, 1998*

Most people in Japan share a national trait whereby they tend to rely on a god in all things. Most households follow one form of faith or another. This person Tojo, though, insisted throughout his life that the god of his own self was superior to all others. His incredible pomposity, arrogance and sense of superiority were far greater than any belief he might have had in a divine being. Simply put, his idea was to say: "There is no God. He's dead. So, follow me, instead."

It was only natural, then, that I would be curious to find out about this person's position and life in the spiritual world. At first, I was not able to meet him. Later, I began to look for him at the direction of True Parents. The thoughts and curiosity of True Parents became my motivation to seek him out.

I had to go into a place where there were no mountains or rivers. As I began to search this area, I couldn't help but wonder whether it was possible for anyone to live there. Then, in one particular place, I began to hear a strange sound, as if someone was moaning in agony. It sounded like he was in a great deal of pain. The sound was coming from a structure that could hardly be called a house. It was more like something that the nomadic peoples in tropical areas of the earth build and then tear down when they eventually move on. I looked more closely, and I began to see signs of human life in this structure. There were a few other structures similar to this one scattered about the area.

I opened the door, which was little more than a piece of tree bark. Inside, I discovered that a few men were using this place to live. One of them was ill. I asked the others whether the man had a headache, but they said they didn't know. I, Sang Hun Lee, said a prayer for them. Then, I placed my hand on the one that was sick, and began to pray for him to be healed.

"I pray in the name of the one who has come as the messenger of God. Let the pain that this man suffers subside," I said. He immediately stopped his moaning and sat up. Then, he asked me, "Who are you that you are able to save me from my suffering?" I asked him to identify himself to me first. He bowed his head, and told me that because I had relieved him of his pain he would consider me to be his teacher, and his god. For this reason, he said, he would tell me what I wanted to know.

"My name is Tojo. While I was on earth, I denied the existence of God. Instead, I claimed that I myself was a god. But when my physical body expired and I came to this place, I discovered that there was no place for me. I tried living in the jungle. I tried going under water. I went many places, but I couldn't find anyone who would was glad to see me. I finally settled here on this barren plain. People are so scarce here that even if I cry out in pain no one knows. Sir, you are my god. Please save me."

I told him that I was errand-boy sent by God. I also told him that my purpose for coming that day was to give him salvation. As soon as I said that, his body began to tremble. He bowed over and over again and thanked me profusely.

I said to him, "The reason I started looking for you was

that the Rev. Sun Myung Moon, who is the True Parent living on earth, told me to come see how you are living here and then convey this information to the people on earth. I received God's permission and came here as quickly as I could."

Tojo said, "The True Parent is your parent, so how is it that he wanted to find me? For what reason did he want to find me?"

I continued to explain to him about True Parents. I told him that the True Parent is not only my physical father but also the messiah at the Second Advent who comes as the father of all people. Tojo wanted to know whether, if the True Parent was the father of all humanity, then could he also be the father a someone like him, Tojo. This was the chance I had been waiting for. I told him, "Yes, that's right. If you just hear the ideas of the Messiah and believe, then you, too, can be his child. He immediately began saying "Thank you, Thank you, Thank you very much" over and over.

I asked if he wanted to hear my lecture, and he said that he would be glad to hear anything that I had to say, because I was the person who had saved him. So, I said I would give him a small lecture right there. I took the content that is normally given over three days and poured it out to him all at once. First, I lectured the content of "The Messiah: His Advent and the Purpose of His Second Coming" and I explained to him the reality of God's existence. Then I poured out the contents of Unification Thought and Victory Over Communism Thought. He seemed totally captivated by the words. Then, he began to cry.

"I, Tojo, deserve to be punished in front of all the people of the world, because I was so arrogant as to put myself in the place of my God." He confessed that he was a sinner among sinners, and asked me to tell him what to do. He asked me to save him. I told him: "Sometime in the future, the Messiah will also come to this world. Until then, let's work together to spread his words." He looked very surprised by this, and said, "If we do that, I will only bring you harm. I you work with me, then you will be attacked, too." He asked it there was any other way that he could be saved. I told him, "This is the only way, so let's wait for the Messiah with a heart of atonement." I asked him to pray, offer expressions of his devotion and assist me in my work. After that, I returned.

## LEADERS OF KOREAN CHRISTIANITY

### KIM HWAL-LAN

Kim Hwal-lan was a very famous woman on earth, who took pride in the fact that she had graduated from the most prestigious academic institutions. She led a life of faith based on certain strong convictions about God, and many people looked up to her as a member of the elite. The question, though, is whether a member of the highest elite on earth can also receive an elite position in the spiritual world.

I visited a club of Christians one day not long after I came to the spiritual world. The people there were waiting earnestly for the Lord to come on the clouds – so much so that they had created an effigy of the Lord and hung it from a cloud. They were praying and expressing their longing for the Lord. I also saw a painting of Jesus there, but Jesus himself was not in the club. There are many such clubs formed by Christians gathering together among themselves.

I visited the clubs, because I was searching for a specific person. Even more than the pain that she had caused the members of our 36 Blessed Couples, I was curious to know the outcome of her erroneous judgements about God. One day, I found her. I came across a woman in a rather unusual club of Christians consisting of members of the upper class. The woman was preaching very energetically, and I went in and listened to what she had to say.

She was saying basically that, since the Lord who is to return had not yet come, it was the responsibility of women to hold candlelight vigils and pray until the day of his coming. We should not be derelict in expressing the devotion of the bride as she waits for her bridegroom, she said. She called on her listeners to join together in prayer until the day of the Lord's return.

I, Sang Hun Lee, stood in the back of the crowd and clapped very loudly. I did so, because I wanted her to notice me so that I might have a chance to meet her. Instead, though, I found that the entire crowd turned around to look at me. Kim Hwal-lan suddenly appeared directly in front of me, and greeted me very politely. I introduced myself as a messenger from God.

She said, "You look like a respectable person, but why do you joke with us? A messenger from God?"

Many people were focusing their attention on me. I continued to lead the conversation in a direction to where I would be able to declare the coming of the Messiah.

"Madam Kim," I said, "the Messiah already returned a long time ago. Your education of brides here is mistaken. I'm sure Jesus knows this, too. The Lord has come. He came a long time ago, and he is working hard for the building of the Kingdom of Heaven, for the establishment of world peace and for the salvation of humanity."

She responded: "That's what the heretics say."

"Then," I continued in a very earnest tone, "will you listen to me while I talk a little about what the heretics say? If you can show me that what I say is mistaken, then I will be glad to study under you."

Most of the people in the crowd were women, and they agreed that they wanted to hear what I had to say. I knew this was my chance. I explained about "The Messiah: His Advent and the Purpose of His Second Coming." I used a detailed historical chart to talk about the parallel providential periods for the coming of the Messiah, and compared it to the present age so that they could understand for themselves that this was the time for his return. I also talked about the issue of Jesus' crucifixion, and how the Lord at the Second Advent would have to carry on the work that Jesus had begun. Then, I put a question to the crowd at large, and particularly to Kim Hwal-lan.

"Am I a fraudulent messenger? Is the content that I have introduced here in error? Doesn't it agree with the general principle? There are many areas of detail. If you like, I can talk about those at another time."

Kim Hwal-lan raised her hand to ask a question. "Why did you come here? Who did you come to see?" I told her that I had come to meet Kim Hwal-lan. Then, I began to talk about True Parents.

I asked her whether she remembered the name, "Sun Myung Moon." She said she did not. I asked her again, but again she said she recalled no one by that name. "In that case," I said, "do you remember hearing about the Unification Church?" She thought for a while, and said that indeed she did recall hearing something about that. I said: "Do you know who is the founder of the Unification Church?" Finally, then, she was able to remember Rev. Moon's name.

"The gentleman who founded the Unification Church is the one who is the Lord at the Second Advent and the True

Parents. He is now shedding his blood and sweat on earth for the sake of human salvation." Kim Hwal-lan's face turned as red as a beat.

"Then, I am a terrible sinner," she said. "Have you come to take me away as a criminal?"

I told her it was not for me to determine whether the term "criminal" applied to her. This is something that only God and Madam Kim herself could judge. The other members of the crowd were very curious. Madam Kim and I were talking about the coming of the Lord at the Second Advent, but they had no way of knowing who we were talking about. Kim Hwal-lan suggested that the two of us meet later in private. I told her then that I would end my lecture for the day. I offered to return the next day, if she wanted, to lecture the Divine Principle. Kim Hwal-lan seemed very dissatisfied with this. She said her group would have a meeting and decide what would be good time for me to come. One woman in the group, though, raised her hand and said: "I want to hear what you have to say. Let's listen to him." Others, then, joined in with her in a chorus of "Let's listen to him. Let's listen to him."

I lectured here for three days. Everyone wept and prayed and sang hymns. We began singing "When the Bridegroom Comes," which is hymn number 162 in the Korean Christian hymnal and has the refrain "Prepare, Prepare." It made quite a ruckus.

Many members on earth, especially those who were forced to terminate their studies at Ehwa Womens University, are interested to know what has become of Kim Hwal-lan. Kim Hwal-lan kept beating her breast with her fists and shouting, "Lord, Lord, what should be done with this sinner? Lord, Lord, please save me, as I am a sinner."

Later, Kim Hwal-lan met with me, and sincerely apologized for what she did on earth. She asked me what she should do for the sake of those who had suffered as a result of her actions. I told her that she should work for the sake of the coming Lord. She should take full charge of the task to go to all women Christians and bear witness that Rev. Sun Myung Moon is the Lord who has come on earth, that he is the True Parents and the Savior, the parents of all humanity. She smiled and said she would do this work to the best of her ability with a heart of atonement. It made me happy to have overcome these people, but I also felt a certain bitterness to think of how they once left a terrible mark on our providential history.

Question: How is it that a person who opposed our will so vehemently is able to live in such tranquility?

Answer: A person who was recognized on earth as an intellectual of the highest order and who served God and made many great efforts during her life is now consigned to a lower realm of the spiritual world where Jesus does not live. Is it accurate, then, to describe this person's position as "tranquil"?

## THE FAMILY OF MARIA PARK

God who rules over all things created spoke as follows: "Sang Hun, it may seem to you that people live according to their own wills, but it is only when the direction of their will is consistent with that of God's will that they can be said to be following a true path. I was curious to know why God had spoken these words to me, and I waited for Him to explain. Then, one day, God told me: "There is a particular place where you must visit today." He then sent a woman of small stature to where I was and told me to go with her. The woman was a messenger of God. Because we were going on God's command, I was especially curious to know where it was that we were going.

The woman told me that the place where God had told me to go and see was not a pleasant place. After we had traveled a certain distance, the woman told me to stop and wait. She called a man to where we were, and invited him to accompany us on our journey. I felt strange in my heart, but I continued to follow along.

Where is this? I could see a large gate that looked similar to the prison gates on earth. It was very high and tightly closed. But then, what is this? After waiting for a long time, the man who had traveled with us said something, and the gate suddenly opened wide. We went in. I could hardly believe what I saw there. The people were all people, but they didn't have the form of normal humans. There were "crying people," "fighting people," "people who have been struck with a sword," "people with crooked eyes," "people biting on a stick," "people with their hands behind their backs," "people with their feet sticking up in the air," "people with blood pouring from their bellies," "people with blood flowing from their ears," "people with malformed hands, feet and ears." The place was filled with people whose appearances are difficult to describe with words. As they moved along, each person kept repeating his or her particular motion, so the group had the appearance of a colony of people suffering from physical disabilities.

This was really strange. I was curious to know why God had sent me to such a place. As I stood there feeling pain in my heart over what I was witnessing, the woman who had come with me called to me and motioned for me to look in a certain direction. "There she is," she said. "The person that God wanted you to see is over there."

I looked in the direction she pointed, and saw a woman

who was holding her lips with her hand. Her hand was stuck to her lips and wouldn't come off. She would try to eat something, but the hand got in the way, and so she would spill more food than she would manage to get into her mouth. I stood in front of the woman and said, "You're Maria Park, aren't you." She nodded her head to tell me I was correct. There were many things I wanted to ask her. But there was no way to do so, because she couldn't open her mouth. I myself was surprised to hear the words "Father, what is to be done with this person" echoing in my heart.

Then, suddenly, the woman began leading me to another place. She pointed out a man who turned out to be Lee Ki-boong. We looked at each other, and I could hardly believe what I saw. Lee Ki-boong had blood pouring from his chest. We were close enough that we could recognize each other. After that, I began looking around on my own. I wanted to find the son of Lee Ki-boong. I wanted to find Lee Kang-suk. How was it possible that an entire family had ended up in such a place? I found the son. He was in a permanent pose of standing behind his father with a knife in his raised hand.

The woman looked at me and suggested we return to God. I offered a prayer to God in this place. "God, please save these people. Please liberate these people before True Parents come here and see them in their present form." No one, though, responded to my prayer. As I traveled back through the large gate, I was thinking: "What is to be done about this gruesome sight? How am I to show this to True Parents?"

I called out to God, and He responded: "Sang Hun, is there pain in your heart?" I just began to cry before God. God told me: "Sang Hun, it's not something for you to cry about. I wanted you to see this, because it's something for which you have to bear responsibility. You must tell my children to live good lives. For the people in that place, the path of salvation will not be easy. Tell my children to live good lives on earth before they come here. Do you understand my meaning? Sang Hun, I'm asking you." Then, God was silent.

## PARK TAE-SUN

When Elder Park was on earth, he was venerated so highly that his authority seemed to rival that of a god. Next, I would like to describe this person's appearance and life in the spiritual world.

I found Elder Park living in a community of regular Christians. The standard of these Christians, though, was not that of faithful people who had lived in attendance of the Lord. Instead, their standard was that of people who had put only a little effort into their faith. So, for example, when they sang hymns or prayed they didn't know the words very well. They were novice believers. Elder Park was among them. I have never conversed with this person. The reason I have not been in a hurry to speak with him is that it is obvious that he is purposely hiding himself in an area that is not appropriate to his position. From what I've seen, I can tell that his faith was based on an arrogant heart, and that he became intoxicated in his mission. In this world, he is living in a place that is considerably distant from God. He still does not understand his position. He lives among novice believers and still holds on to his past domain. I will let some more time pass before meeting him.

Next is the life of regular Christian ministers. In the Christian realm that I have seen, I have not come across anything remarkable with regard to ministers. I have not found a situation where a minister who was specially revered on earth has been given a special position here. What I have noticed is that even if a person is given the position of minister on earth, here he may not have that position. I have not yet seen the ministers who opposed us. In hell, or in the place that is called Heaven, there is no sign indicating where the ministers are, so I have not been able to find them. This is something that I am planning to do in the future.

# KOREA'S POLITICAL LEADERS

## SYNGMAN RHEE

I was curious to find out about how people who had been president of a country were living in the spiritual world. Here, a person doesn't receive a large residence just because he was president of his country, so it's difficult to find these people unless you really look for them. I decided to use an unusual method in order to find President Syngman Rhee. As I meditated, I prayed: "God, please lead my heart to wherever President Rhee lives." At a particular spot, I began to hear very beautiful singing. It caught my attention to the extent that I started heading in the direction of the sound. After a while, the singing stopped. I stood for a while, wondering how to continue my search, and I finally decided to just try on my own. The place was surrounded on four sides by mountains, though, and this made it difficult to see where things were.

I decided to put my trust in the general direction that I had followed in order to arrive at this place, and began looking around that area. Once in a while, people would come and go from the woods. I wasn't sure whom I should ask, and so I just kept searching the area. Soon, I noticed a man sitting at a bend in the road, apparently in deep thought. I went to him to get a good look at him, but he wasn't Syngman Rhee. I asked him whether he had ever heard of someone named President Syngman Rhee nearby. He answered me in a way that I thought odd. He said: "I don't know if he's a president or what, but someone lives in that house across the road there."

I went to the house, thinking there was a chance I might find President Rhee there. The house was a little bit better than most homes. Oddly, though, it was very quiet, and I didn't see any signs that someone lived there. Inside, there was no sign of anyone. I was looking around inside the house, when finally I heard someone make a noise. It turned out to be President Syngman Rhee. I was very surprised to see how he was dressed. His clothes were very shabby. His appearance was scruffy, and he had no one with him.

I quickly greeted him: "You must be President Syngman Rhee. My name is Sang Hun Lee." He wanted to know how I had known where to find him. I told him that God had sent me, and he asked me if I had ever met God.

I said, "Yes, I met Him."

"Why, then, has such a great person come here?" he asked.

I asked him why it was that a former president was living such a lonely life in this place. He said he didn't know the reason himself. He told me that he had a large house in another place nearby, but he lived here because he was more comfortable. He told me that since he couldn't be treated the way he wanted, he felt more comfortable living in a place where he didn't have to meet anyone.

"Well, yes," I said, "but this is a place where neither God nor Jesus are present. Do you have to live here?"

He replied, "God and Jesus have forsaken me." But he also said that he wanted to meet God and Jesus. When this man who was responsible for a nation failed to fulfill his responsibility, he heard his own people demand that he give up his office and was thrown out of office. Seen from the perspective of eternal life, Syngman Rhee's life is nothing more than the result of his failure to fulfill his responsibility, either during his tenure as president or during his life as a human being. I have not done so yet, but someday I plan to invite him, too, to my home and talk to him about True Parents.

*All the people who now live far below the stations that they enjoyed in the physical world are people who were traitors to the providence, and I think that the place where they exist now is none other than hell.

## LETTERS
### A LETTER PRESENTED BY JESUS
### TO TRUE PARENTS                              *MAY 22, 1998*

Father, my name is Jesus. Though I am not worthy, you have given me so much love, concerned yourself for my sake, and prayed for me so often. Even this is such a tremendous blessing for me, and yet you have even given my wife a home that is far more than she deserves. How can I ever repay you for all your kindness?

Father!
My wife is a woman who is far better than I deserve. Truly, I am awestruck. From this point on, my wife and I will uphold your will and work to make an offering of our lives as a beautiful family. I will attend Heung-jin Nim, offer my prayers and hard work for the sake of the direction of the True Parents and

the providence of restoration.

Also, Father! There is a vast number of Christians here, but their hearts have been closed. Now, you have narrowed the gap between us and Heung-jin Nim, who is able to establish the same flow of cooperative relations as on earth. We will work hard now on the basis of this spiritual backing and foundation.

The name of "Jesus" is always being made to stand out on earth, and no words can describe how ashamed I feel before you, Father, because of this.

Father, please forgive this sinner (in the sense that the responsibility was not fulfilled). Some day, your resentment will be resolved. Christians on earth will begin to have dreams about the wretched appearance of Jesus in the spiritual world.

Father! I truly thank you. I love my wife. Thank you.

I pray that the Parents may have long life and good health.

Jesus, who was born in Nazareth of Judea sends this letter from the spiritual world to Father.

*I am very sorry, Mrs. Kim, to trouble you so often. (This is in reference to the letter that I sent to Mr. Chang.)

## A LETTER PRESENTED BY CHOONG-MO NIM TO TRUE PARENTS

Father, this is your mother.

Father, how many difficulties you must have faced over the years? As a result of my inadequacies, you were not able to go a smooth course, and you are left with no choice but to live a life where there is no difference between night and day. Father, it always pains me to know that you have had to suffer, because you lacked the foundation of your mother's devotion.

Father! Together with Daemo-Nim, I am learning many things and teaching many things. Whenever you think it necessary, I am willing to assist. Am I being too arrogant? Is it still too early?

Father! I will become a loyal mother, or "choong-mo," according to the title you have given me. And, Father, the image of me wearing a towel over my head is very unattractive, isn't it? It causes you shame, doesn't it? I have asked this lady to remove the towel, because I'm afraid that image will cause you embarrassment.

Father! Please wait and see. I truly will become a loyal mother. Father, Mother, I pray and pray again for your long life and good health.

*As she writes this letter, she is crying again. Whenever she appears, she is crying.

## A LETTER PRESENTED BY YOUNG-SOON TO TRUE PARENTS

I present this letter to Father.
Father!
This is Kim Young-soon. I dare to present this letter to you. I received your instructions from Rev. Kwak, and in the car on the way home I was feeling the weight of the task, because I didn't know what to do. Then, I received God's encouragement to "Be joyful that you have been blessed." I felt I had to offer devotion. I thought I would offer 40 days. Then, I wanted to make it 21 days, and then 3 days. The longer the period of devotion, the longer you would have to wait. The next day, I received a phone call from Rev. Kwak. He told me that he was leaving for the United States in three days, and he needed me

to give him all the results of your instructions before then. I was at a loss. Oh God, help me. How can I complete everything in three days? God, please, please help me. How can I do this in three days? Then, suddenly, I heard a voice say: "Mrs. Kim, this is Sang Hun Lee. Don't you know Father's character? Let's begin this evening. I'm ready. Then, he gave me a list of the prayer items. I told him that I didn't even know who "Japan's Tojo" was, but he told me not to worry. He said he knew about Tojo well, so I didn't have worry that I didn't know him. He was very calm and kept encouraging me. He never comes unless it is for a public purpose. Yet, when Father's instructions are involved, he comes immediately. I realized how deep the communication is between a father and son. The spiritual world that cannot be seen with the physical eye, . . . I am learning many things, and feeling many things.

Father!